THE INFLUENCE OF SAINT BE

A

Initial B containing St Bernard standing with book and staff. In the margin a praying nun, 'Mathildis'. From Keble College, Oxford, MS. 49 *(see Note on p. vi)*

THE INFLUENCE OF SAINT BERNARD

Anglican Essays with an Introduction by

Jean Leclercq OSB

EDITED BY

SISTER BENEDICTA WARD SLG

SLG PRESS
Fairacres
OXFORD

*We dedicate these studies of Saint Bernard to
our brothers in Christ in the Cistercian Order
and to Dom Jean Leclercq OSB
'amicus Bernardi et noster'*

© THE COMMUNITY OF THE SISTERS OF THE LOVE OF GOD 1976

ISBN 0 7238 0061 3
ISSN 0307-1405

CONTENTS

INTRODUCTION
Jean Leclercq OSB
page vii

BERNARD AND AFFECTIVE MYSTICISM
Andrew Louth
page 1

CONTEMPLATION AND ACTION
IN THE PASTORAL THEOLOGY OF ST BERNARD
Martin Smith SSJE
page 11

THREE STYLES OF MONASTIC REFORM
Rowan Williams
page 23

ST BERNARD AND ST GILBERT
Brian Golding
page 41

THE KNIGHTS OF GOD
CITEAUX AND THE QUEST OF THE HOLY GRAIL
Sister Isabel Mary SLG
page 53

BERNARD AND ABELARD
Sister Edmée SLG
page 89

APOPHTHEGMATA BERNARDI
SOME ASPECTS OF ST BERNARD OF CLAIRVAUX
Sister Benedicta Ward SLG
page 135

NOTE ON THE SEAL OF ST BERNARD

In a letter to Pope Eugenius (ep.284), written c. 1151, Bernard writes:

I have been in perils amongst false brethren, and many letters have been forged, and fraudulently sealed with my seal, and have gone forth into many different hands, and my chief fear is that this treachery may have reached even to you. This is why I am forced to discontinue the use of my former seal, and to use this new one, which you notice is fresh, containing both my device and my name.

In the same volume as this letter (*Life and Works of St Bernard*, trans. by Samuel Eales from Mabillon, Vol.II) there is a full account of this seal and of the 'happy circumstance' whereby this 'inestimable piece of antiquity' came into the hands of the Director of the Museum of Antiquities at Rouen in 1837. 'I owe it [he writes] to the generosity of a retired officer, M. Pays of Issoudon, who wrote: "This seal was bought from a second-hand salesman, who became possessed in 1790 of the old copper articles of the Collegiate Church of St Cyr, of Issoudun, which was affiliated to Clairvaux." '

NOTE ON THE FRONTISPIECE

The frontispiece comes from a Legendary according to Dominican use, made for the convent of Dominican nuns at Heiligen Kreuz in Regensburg, Germany, shortly after 1271. The nun 'Mathildis' was a member of the convent at that time.

The half-tone plate printed in this book has been taken from a colour slide made by the Bodleian Library from Keble College, MS.49, and is reproduced here by kind permission of the Warden and Fellows of Keble College, Oxford.

INTRODUCTION

by Jean Leclercq OSB

Bernard of Clairvaux is a world in himself, and one that has still not been fully explored. Not only articles but books appear on him every year. A section of these are reprints of older works which, even if they made history when first published, as did C. Butler's *Western Mysticism*, are no longer up to date after half a century of new research. Others are full of personal and sentimental interpretations, some of which may be pious, but which lack any scientific basis. Others are of a technical, highly specialized nature. The present Fairacres Publication, continuing the standard of the excellent series to which it belongs, has cleared a path for itself between all these boulders: it has weight, it is full of learning, and at the same time it nourishes faith and stimulates love for the Church. Moreover, nothing is lost by the fact that it is a pleasure to read.

Faced with the tide of publications on Bernard which flood in on us, one sometimes wonders if anything new will yet be said, and it must be admitted that this is not always the case. Here, however, there really is new matter, both in approach and in avenues of research, and that not only hypothetically but in fact. Anyone who knows Oxford and Fairacres will not be surprised. Behind all these essays, it is possible to discern the discreet, inspiring presence of that great student of the twelfth century, Sir Richard Southern. The Community of the Sisters of the Love of God shows here to the full, through the agency of a few of its members who represent the rest, its special combination of ability and zeal. Familiarity with the patristic, liturgical, and monastic background, and knowledge of secular literature both ancient and modern are expressed in a lucid and eirenic style, which bears witness to an existence unified by the contemplative religious life and inspired by the spirituality of a great ecclesial tradition. Joy, humour, at times '*un certain charme féminin*' also help to make the product of such a 'school of charity' an authentic continuation of the humanism of the great religious orders of the Middle Ages and of the Renaissance. Finally, I cannot fail to pay tribute to a friend who was to me, as to so many others, a guide and inspiring example, Dom David Knowles, whose invisible presence can also be discerned behind all the pages we are about to read. From the days long ago when I used to go to see him at Peterhouse, Cambridge, up to the last visits I paid him in Hampshire, through his letters, and in the opportunities which he offered me of working with him, I have always admired this incomparable scholar and faithful monk of God for remaining so simply and so deeply human. He gave us the example of someone full of all kinds of riches, but whose heart was not divided.

After paying this sincere tribute to a few friends, I must introduce this collection of studies on St. Bernard. The aim of this presentation is certainly not to summarize them, or to pass judgement on them, but to share certain reactions on reading them. Of course, they do not touch on all the aspects of St. Bernard's personality, nor on all the fields of his activity. But one can say that they shed light on the essential aspects of his character and work, in so far as by discussing precise examples, they lead us to a deeper understanding of the relations of Bernard with God and with human society, both secular and monastic, with special reference—as one might rightly hope—to England.

BERNARD AND GOD

Can one separate Bernard's attitude to God from that which he has to human beings? It was God Himself who drove Bernard back to men, and it was both the experience of what was human in himself, and compassion for men received through grace, that provided the starting-point for his development both in prayer and in service. The merit of Andrew Louth's essay is that it enables us to have done with a facile and fallacious dichotomy between love of God and love of neighbour. Not only are they compatible but, according to Bernard, they are one: they are the expression of the same need to come out of oneself, to give oneself to others, which continues in man a movement which begins in God. 'Love is a great thing, but only if it comes back to its principle, if it returns to its origin, if, pouring itself back into its source, it there continually draws the means wherewith to flow continually.' (Sup. Cant. 83, 4.) This total love of God and of human persons is not the monopoly of monks and nuns living under the vow of celibacy. The psychologists with whom I have been working recently on the treatise *On the Love of God* insisted on the fact that Bernard's teaching could just as well be lived out in marriage. Reading this text for the first time, 'naively' so to speak, without prejudice, they drew from it the conviction that what mattered to Bernard was the integration of the whole being with the action of grace which sanctifies all human activities that accord with that 'law of God', called elsewhere by Bernard 'His voice', that interior demand which God has placed in man made in His image and which He continually restores in man, giving him thereby the possibility of realizing himself. It would be possible to translate the anthropology of Bernard in terms of modern psychology. A similar capacity for the integration of all human love which is in accord with the divine demand, into the actual love of God, is less apparent in William of St Thierry. The latter, if he is perhaps more profound, is also more systematic. In the measure that he sometimes appears to make his anthropological schema correspond with the distinction between various states of monastic life, it is possible that, for him, total effective integration is the monopoly of those living in religious celibacy.

Another irritating dichotomy, which Martin Smith helps us to avoid, is that which opposes action and contemplation. In reality, it is a question of priorities, not of exclusions. At a time when the attraction of 'immediacy' is so strong, it is good to hear it reaffirmed that, for Bernard, as for all the great spiritual masters, the first priority, if one can use such a term, belongs to 'contemplative prayer'—to use a formula dear to Dom John Chapman, and which seems less pretentious, less ambitious and less discouraging than the word 'contemplation'; for does not the latter at once evoke exceptionally lofty mystical states? Bernard was speaking of 'consideration', borrowing from the New Testament a word of which Martin Smith brings out the whole content. Bernard was using this term for the benefit of a monk who had become a man of action, but whose teaching and conduct were to reflect, to radiate, his own union with God. In this, Bernard is in accord with the doctrine which was to be St. Thomas's in his last period, that of the end of the *Summa Theologica* where at that moment of full maturity, free from previous theories—those of others and even his own—he rejects the idea of a 'mixed' life. There can only be unified lives in which the leading direction, the priority, allows for excursions and detours which are not deviations, and of exceptions which may be frequent but which never become a general principle of conduct or a programme of action planned in advance and justified afterwards. In theology as in practice, there is only one logic, that of love, which brings all back to itself as to the centre from which it has set out. Once again, one thinks of that Bernardine law: 'Love is a great thing, as long as it comes back to its principle . . .' The activities of contemplative life and service are not like parallel lines between which there may be 'minglers' or bridges, but which never meet in themselves. They are concentric circles, all setting out from the same spiritual experience, and bringing back to it both the one who has received the experience and those with whom he has shared it. Thus inner unity demands universality, for it necessarily leads to it. Did Bernard really feel such tension between the two as he sometimes says—and says not without a certain rhetorical exaggeration? He could not help being a vigourous writer, and he could fall victim to one or another of his formulas if he took them all literally. However, there was also in him, and he expected it in his readers, a streak of humour—which, fortunately, is never lacking in this volume. In him, seriousness is often tempered with a smile. If it is true that at times he forcefully expresses a tension which he experiences intensely at the 'surface level' of his psychology, his work taken as a whole leads us to realize that he also enjoyed—and that habitually—a profound unity.

BERNARD AND MONASTICISM

This is the field of Bernard's human relationships, and we are led into its inner meaning by Rowan Williams. In the poem which bears the title *Occupatio*, Odo of Cluny had explicitly given his Order—which was not a reform but a new beginning, a sort of creation—the aim of reviving in the Church the effects of the mystery of Pentecost. There has been and is only one Pentecost, and the explosive experience which accompanied its beginnings can become serene and comfortable to the point of resembling sleep, if not death. There are times in the Church's history, therefore, when renewal must appear to consist in innovation. In this sense the initiative of the founders of Cîteaux stands in direct line of descent from that of the founders and first abbots of Cluny. Even the eleventh-century abbots succeeded in keeping for what they called *le corps clunisien*, which had expanded so much, something of its youthfulness, of that enthusiasm through which it was able both to influence the Gregorian reform without losing its freedom, and to preserve its own liturgical tradition, maintaining its flexibility and rhythm, yet introducing into it an element of devotion and spontaneous expression. All these points are constantly having fresh light thrown on them by recent works.[1]

The idea of Benedict as a new Moses, because he promulgated a code of legislation adapted for those Christians who are monks, did not remain the monopoly of an Odo of Cluny. The idea is equally attested, and with precision, in Bernard and other Cistercians.[2] It raises the whole problem of the value of the Benedictine Rule and, in general, of any rule for Religious. That is why it is not only of historical interest; it is relevant today. Moreover, in the past, the question was asked just as much about other bodies of legislation—those of St Augustine, St Basil, the Institutions of the Friars— as it was asked about the Rule of St Benedict. What is it, then, to live according to a Rule? Since I have expressed my views on this subject elsewhere,[3] here it will be sufficient to summarize the results obtained from examining forms of Profession and various other documents.

Paradoxically, one could say that it is more important to have a Rule than to practise it; for the Rule points to the theory, while its practical working out is fixed by what is called successively 'the customary', 'the institution', and 'the constitutions'. The Rule fixes the general orientation in a particular kind of life, for example that of the Eastern monks, of the Western monks, of the Canons Regular, or of the apostolic orders which appeared in the thirteenth century. Within each of these major orientations, in line with each of these directions, a thirteenth-century pope, Innocent IV, could affirm that the Rule of St Benedict—and he could have said the same of others—is binding only with regard to 'the essential elements of all Religious life'. Reference to one of the great ancient Rules fixes a classification, allows the characterization of a type of life, and confirms its authenticity, but it does not impose the particular observances that the document contained when it was drawn up, in circumstances which are not those of other times and places. Thus, for Western monks and nuns, the Rule of St. Benedict is both necessary and of only relative authority: necessary, because it determines that way of living in the Church which is monastic life; of relative authority because it is not adequate for laying down in detail how, in practice, this monastic life is to be led, nor for fixing its observances. It places a group of Christians in a tradition, that of monasticism, which differs from other ways of giving oneself to God and serving the Church in Religious life. It simply inculcates a spirit, and shows which are the spiritual values which distinguish the monk from those who lead the Christian life in a different, and often better, way than his. The Cistercians therefore enjoyed the same freedom towards St. Benedict's Rule as did the Cluniac monks, and they did not hesitate to put it into practice. Of them as of the others, both in the past and in the present, the formula is valid, according to which one *follows* the Rule, but does not *practise* it. That is the only really traditional way of *observing* it, the only way which is common to all monks and to all nuns, and which is adequate to its greatness. For a Rule is more and better than a regulation.

Brian Golding's highly accurate study takes us into the field of the influences exercised by Bernard in countries which he did not visit, but influenced through so many men drawn to the brilliance of Clairvaux itself, or who were in institutions which were not Bernard's own, but which drew inspiration from his writings. This was the case with the Black monks of St Denis, of Chartres, and elsewhere, with the regular Canons, with the Templars, and with those groups of hermits with whom his relationship was the subject of fresh investigations about ten years ago;[4] his interest in the eremitical movement of his time provides a theme which recurs many times in that work. With Gilbert of Sempringham, Bernard also shared the idea of welcoming more women into monastic life, and from all walks of life. Like Fontevrault and other new foundations of the twelfth century, Cîteaux did not look favourably on the establishment of monasteries for the nobility, from which the daughters of the common people, of the peasants and the bourgeois, were excluded. It is true that, like Gilbert, and earlier than him, Bernard imposed on them very strict enclosure. This can be seen in the statutes which he 'advised' the abbot of Molesmes to draw up for the nuns of Jully.[5]

BERNARD AND SOCIETY

Can one really speak of incompatibility between the life of monks and nuns, for which Bernard did so much, and that of chivalry, from which he received and used so many images—as I hope to demonstrate elsewhere—and on which he had such great influence, as we see confirmed in the admirable article by Sister Isabel Mary? For living in married love can also be a life which admits of no half measures. In his writings, Bernard rejects adultery, concubinage, any form of sexual license, and just as strongly does he defend marriage, making it the symbol and even the model for all loves: that of God for humanity, that of the Church for Christ, that of any Christian who becomes one spirit with God, 'as husband and wife become two persons in one flesh'. Shortly after Bernard had finished his sermons on the Song of Songs, Chrétien de Troyes, in the same region in which everyone was still talking of the abbot of Clairvaux, wrote his first romance, which set the tone for all his subsequent work and for the whole Grail cycle: it was *Eric and Enid*, which is an exaltation of conjugal fidelity.

Moreover, the hazardous life of an Eric or a Galahad on the one hand, and the life of a monk on the other, is seen to have in common the search for a form of life which is exacting, or even heroic. Even in recent times, it is an historical fact that after every war there is a rush to the cloister. And, indeed, when a man has known the exaltation which gives him a measure of self-transcendence, a going beyond what he would have thought himself capable of in times of ease, can he ever again be content with a life of mediocrity? Religious and monastic life is a great adventure: no one knows through what trials, what tests, what detours God will make a man pass in order to lead him to Himself. And can one not say the same of married love which remains—as one must constantly reaffirm against certain commonplaces inherited from the late nineteenth century—the model of *normal* medieval love, that is to say, not only conforming to the norms laid down by the Church, but in fact the most frequent form of love. This is not the place to insist on this *fact*, which I hope to set forth elsewhere, and on the subject of which I already have the support of eminent specialists in the history of love.

In the twelfth century, the 'spiritual man' was not identified, any more than he was in St. Paul or is today, with the monk. The whole of society was to be made an 'imperium of Love', as Sister Isabel Mary so attractively puts it. Now there is only one language of love, one might dare to say that there is only one experience of it, undergone at various levels, by various men and women, who may, in any case, be successively the same persons: young knights, or converted clerks who have become monks, masters of sacred doctrine who have become lay-brothers, 'bourgeois' and peasants sometimes entrusted with important functions; this was what made up twelfth-century monastic society in the new Orders which were recruited among adults. Was this a society whose experience of love was opposed to that of monastic society? Monks and nuns on the one hand, others who were in love on the other, were different, distinct, even kept apart; were they alienated from one another, fixed in superimposed social strata as though the former were superior to the latter? Is not legitimate secular love rather simply 'transposed' to the level of monastic love? The same song, played on the same human instrument, but on two key-boards, in two registers; the same melody, but two harmonies? The one is not necessarily more beautiful than the other to the ear of the only listener whose judgement matters: God who created every man, from whom comes all grace, to whom leads every generous human response which is in conformity with the example and teaching of His incarnate Son; He who remains present and acts among us through His Spirit. 'A noble creature is man', Bernard affirms. It is every human person, both men and women, and it is the whole of human nature which is noble. The love of God in a unified humanity—an integrated humanity, psychologists would say today—is not an ideal inaccessible to those living outside the cloister. Certainly monastic love is a model for all; but it is not a sociological model, implying that one must shut oneself away in order to love God and His creatures without half measures. Rather, it is a moral and religious model, acting as a pointer or, like the Rule, as an arrow pointing to a path on which each will set out according to his vocation and the grace given. Is one then interpreting Bernard with personal optimism if one admires the 'reality' of his message for the world of his time with its highly varied society, and if one thinks that monasticism and secular society—that of chivalry and otherwise—were more interrelated than is often stated?

BERNARD AND ABELARD

I hesitate to say anything about Abelard in only a few sentences when so many over-simplifications already abound concerning this complex man and the confused times in which he lived. Sister Edmée's perceptive article discusses some of the aspects of this vast problem.

It is too often forgotten that between Abelard and Bernard there was a third person, William of St Thierry, who, distressed by the former, pushed the latter into action. William was a vigorous thinker, combining richness of 'personality' with an extraordinary depth of 'being'. Each of the three felt himself responsible for 'circles' of disciples and former pupils for whom, above all, he wrote. Each of the three had supporters and opponents in various parts of the country, but especially in Paris and at Rome. The detailed studies on the chronology of this whole conflict being carried out by P. Zerbi, and of which the most recent is the one prepared by him for the St Thierry Colloqium of October 1976, constantly draw attention to this political background.

How, then, is one personally to decide whose side one is on out of the three—and does one have to? Posterity has, at any rate, decided overwhelmingly, if the evidence from the number of surviving manuscripts suggests a verdict. Of Abelard's correspondence—assuming it is authentic—the first extant manuscript dates from more than a hundred years after him, and there are very few copies thereafter. In the same period, and with the same chances of texts disappearing, we have six hundred manuscripts of St Bernard, while the later copies cannot be counted. For Abelard, on the other hand, the tradition is weak, even in the case of his sermons which are not lacking in spiritual vigour, although they bear the tone of rhetoric rather than that of experience. In regard to his doctrinal works, the premature death of E. Buytaert has left part of Abelard's *Theologia scholarium* unedited, and the position is further obscured by the fact that some of his teachings, even manuscripts of his known works, are lacking. One is thus reduced to the statements of his disciples, buried in the footnotes of A. Landgraf's *Frühscholastik*. Is there, moreover, any coherence between these doctrinal works and the correspondence? One can do no more than guess. And yet the *Golden Letter*, written by William of St Thierry to protect the vocation of the young Carthusians of Mont-Dieu who were feeling the impact of Abelardian ideas, has survived in several hundred copies. And if St Bernard's letter-treatise against Abelard exists in 117 manuscripts it is not because there was much interest, before the nineteenth century, in the controversy which was to lead to the Council of Sens; it is because it contains pages full of teaching and fervour concerning Jesus Christ and the mysteries he revealed. It is because it contains food for love.

Among the vicissitudes of today and tomorrow one thing is certain: that which is constant through every crisis—in spite of all exegesis—is the Word of God. That which will continue to feed our faith are the texts which have been, and can still be, the object of *lectio divina*. Intellectuals can bring to bear on them a light that is provisional and liable to be superseded; that is their function and their duty. But nothing will replace the 'language of fire' of an Augustine or of a Bernard—and the learning of the universities can never extinguish that flame.

Apophthegmata Bernardi

With the learned and unassuming pages of Sister Benedicta Ward we come to that which provides the key to the whole mystery that was and is St Bernard, the key to his personality and to his attraction both in the past and in the present: his joy. Sister Benedicta has gathered a few echoes of it in the literature she knows so well—that of the miracles. There are other echoes, in great number, among those who recorded his life, and firstly in his own writings. In fact, the 'sayings' of Bernard were collected, like those of Antony and of Anselm. There are some in Geoffrey of Auxerre's reminiscences of him;[6] there are 200 pages of them in the second part of volume six of the new edition of his works. Several of these 'sentences' were already to be found in the editions of Mabillon and Migne which are still quoted; but a new series, the longest, can now be added to those on which one could already draw. Some of the 'sentences' are very brief; many are three lines long, others only two. Some consist of six words, or even of five. In them a whole monastic wisdom, which has been lived, is condensed into formulas of which the spice or the flavour comes from reminiscences of the Bible, the Rule of St Benedict, or other fundamental documents.

Did the Abbot of Clairvaux not make his monks smile when he told them that the four kinds of monk, good and bad, that St Benedict begins by describing, are to be found in every community?[7] And did he not smile himself when expounding what has been summarized as follows, and which he presents as a sort of riddle: 'Our feet should be like hind's feet, and like the calf's'? (*Pedes nostri esse debent sicut cervorum, et sicut vituli.* Sent. II, 44.) What does this mean? Scripture says several times that the feet of hinds are agile, run, rise up towards the heights (Ps. 17:34 (or 18:33)), whereas those of calves are always supposed to move but little and remain in the plains. Is it possible to reconcile freedom of spirit and stability? I leave it to you, St Bernard seems to say.

A little further on, with other biblical reminiscences, he praises the paradoxical wisdom of God, which reconciles things which seem contradictory to men:

> The wisdom of God, like a partridge, feeds young which she has not born; like a hen, she gathers her chickens under her wings; like an eagle, she forces them to flight. (Sent. II, 47.)

> A driver of oxen must have two things: a sweet voice, to soften the labour of those who toil; the prick of a goad, to rouse the torpor of those who flag. (Sent. II, 70.)

> (*Bulbucus habere debet duo: vocis suavitatem, quae laborem mulceat operantium: aculei punctionem, quae torporem excutiat pigritantium.*)

Here again, as in so many sayings of the Fathers, the point is to show that grace can join in unity what reason opposes.

> God's dish is small, but it contains three courses: a splendour of clarity which will shine as the sun; a wholeness of purity which will be

as the angels; a steadfast eternity which will be like God. (Sent. II, 129.) *(In scutella Dei tria fercula continentur: claritatis perspicuitas, quae fulgebit ut sol; integritas puritatis, quarent ut angeli; firmitas aeternitatis, quae erit ut Deus.)*
Here, to the playfulness of the images, is added the interaction of the sounds; to the poetry is added verbal musicality.

A good and easy conscience belongs to the perfect; a good and uneasy conscience to the imperfect; a bad and uneasy conscience to beginners; and a bad and easy conscience to the completely hardened. (Sent. III, 58.)

The foundations are invisible: they are Christ and our call to sanctification. The roof is equally hidden: it is the hope of our reward, which is in heaven. (Sent. III, 110.)

One could multiply these examples of discreet humour. Is not joy the sign of a unified being? Who is more happy than God who is without doubt the most unified of all? And is this unity not another name for love? In the last book of his last work, *De Consideratione*, Bernard was often to ask the question, 'What is God?' and to answer it with precision as well as with depth and with reverence for the mystery of it. How had he been led to such a 'finale'? One imagines him, for instance, at Paris, towards 1140, talking to the students, of whom some, like Geoffrey of Auxerre, were 'converted' and followed him to Clairvaux. One knows the major importance of questions relating to the Trinity and to the attributes of God in the teaching of Abelard, and in the controversies which surrounded him there. One pictures the young clerics trying to catch out this abbot who had emerged from his cloister. But in a commentary on the Song of Songs attributed in the manuscripts to Helinand of Froidmont or Odo of Cheriton, there happens to be a very brief anecdote about the period, of which the last word is in itself a striking apophthegm: 'It is said that Blessed Bernard was once asked in the schools what God was. He replied, Love.'[8]

* * * * *

NOTES

1. In English there has appeared Bede Lackner's book, *Eleventh Century Background of Citeaux*, Washington D.C., 1972. To make up for the impression that linguistic

barriers still prevent a common market of texts and ideas, may I be permitted to mention at least two publications: *Cluny Bertrage zu Gestalt und Wirkung der Cluniazensischen Reform*, edited by Helmut Richter, Darmstadt 1975 (13 articles and 14 pages of bibliography). *Il monachesimo e la reforma ecclesiastica (1049-1122)*, Milan 1971.

2. See Vol. III of *Recueil d'études sur S. Bernard*, Rome 1969, pp. 279-285. where I have given the references.

3. *Qu'est-ce que vivre selon une Règle?* in *Collecteana Cisterciensia*, 32 (1970), pp. 155-163, reprinted in *Moines et Moniales ont-ils un avenir?* Bruxelles-Paris 1971, pp. 131-142.

4. *L'eremitismo in Occidente nei secoli XI e XII*, Milan 1965, pp. 573-580; on the hermit movement in England, ibid., pp. 271-310, where H. Dauphin expounds the work of J. Dickinson, R. Foreville, and others.

5. I have published this text in *Études sur S. Bernard et le texte de ses écrits*. Rome (*Analecta S. Ord. Cisterciensis*, IX, 1-2) 1953, pp. 193-4.

6. *Les Souvenirs inédits de Geoffroy d'Auxerre sur S. Bernard*, in *Études sur S. Bernard*, loc. cit., pp. 151-170.

7. Sent. III, 35; cf. *The Love of Learning and the Desire for God*, third edition, New York 1974, p. 210, where I have quoted the text as evidence of Cistercian humour.

8. I have edited this text under the title *Hélinand de Froidmont ou Odon de Chériton?* in *Archives d'histoire doctrinale et littéraire du moyen âge*, Vol. 44 for the year 1965, published Paris 1966.

BERNARD AND AFFECTIVE MYSTICISM

Andrew Louth

IN HIS *WESTERN MYSTICISM* Abbot Butler discusses the mysticism of Augustine, Gregory, and Bernard, and finds with them a form of mysticism which he wishes to be seen as manifesting classical restraint and sobriety. We have the priority of the contemplative life, though not its isolation from the active life, and this contemplative life directed towards the vision of God which is reserved for heaven, but may be fleetingly attained in this life. The experience of rapture is known, but no stress is laid on experience of trance, visions, etc. It is a mysticism of light, not a mysticism of darkness. It is non-Dionysian mysticism (in both senses of the word, so to speak). It certainly seems to be the case that the mysticism of Augustine, Gregory, and Bernard is innocent of any Dionysian taint (as Butler would see it)—that is, of any awareness of the writings of the Pseudo-Areopagite. Although if, as Gilson believes, Bernard is influenced by Erigena's translation of Maximus the Confessor, it seems odd that he should be unaware of the same Erigena's translation of Pseudo-Dionysius. Nevertheless, there is no very convincing sign of such influence. Whether this accounts for the contrast between the mysticism of Bernard and his predecessors and later 'Dark Night' mysticism is not so clear. (David Knowles' doubts can be found in his contribution to Gordon Rupp's *Festschrift*[1]). However, that is not our concern here. Our concern has more to do with the consistency of Dom Butler's classical, non-Dionysian concept of western mysticism; and in particular how justly Bernard can be found within a tradition that Augustine appears to have initiated.

There is no doubt that Bernard is deeply indebted to Augustine; there are many parallels and they are not superficial. But there is much contrast. An example would be the way in which for Bernard the mystical life (it might be truer to say the monastic life) is a progression, a ladder, the summit of which is an experience of rapture which, fleeting in this life, is a foretaste of heaven. Augustine, of course, knows about progress in the spiritual life and, like Bernard delights in constructing 'ladders' to climb in that life. He also knows about rapture. But whereas rapture is habitually found to characterize the topmost rung of Bernard's ladders, this is not so with Augustine. *De Trinitate* which, in its second part, is perhaps his most mature and important exposition of the soul's ascent to God, does not discuss rapture. But is this significant? And, if so, what does it signify? For Augustine the goal of the soul's quest is to know God, and knowing him to love him. Even in the rapture he describes in *Confessions*, IX. x, it is a moment of understanding (*momentum intellegentiae*) attained by swift thought (*rapida cogitatione*). For Bernard, rapture is a supremely intense delight felt by the soul for the sweetness (*suavitas*) of God, a delight that overwhelms the soul. 'When a feeling (*affectum*) of this kind is experienced, the soul, drunk with the divine love, forgetful of self, and seeming to itself a broken vessel, goes out completely into God, and cleaving to God becomes one spirit with him . . .'[2] 'To feel thus is to be deified', he says a little later on (*sic affici, deificari est*).[3] Rapture assumes prominence in Bernard's mysticism because feeling is prominent; for rapture is, presumably, a supremely *felt* experience.

Any religiously significant mysticism is a mysticism of love—and both Bernard and Augustine are exponents of such a mysticism. Both are concerned with the purifying and deepening of the soul's love of God. For Augustine, however, the soul's love of God and the soul's knowledge of God go together: the soul wants to know God more and more because it loves him, and loves him because it knows that he is supreme Truth and Beauty. Love and knowledge of God are united in the kind of knowledge we have of God, namely, wisdom, *sapientia*. *Sapientia*, in contrast to *scientia*, ordinary knowledge, is concerned with eternal reality and contemplation of it; *scientia* is concerned with particular, passing things and their use, and so is more active than contemplative. With Bernard, however, there is a sharp contrast between knowledge and love, for love is not primarily a desire for possession and delight in possessing, as with Augustine, but a feeling. *Amor est affectio naturalis, una de quattuor*—'Love is a feeling, one of four'[4] (the others being fear, joy, and sorrow). Whereas you can have an intellectual desire, feeling is different from knowing. With Augustine, Bernard sees wisdom, *sapientia*, as perfecting the soul's love of God. But this agreement over words disguises a total contrast of meaning. *Sapientia* is not for Bernard contemplation of eternal reality, but *sapor boni*, a *taste* for the good.[5] When he contrasts *sapientia* and *scientia* he is not contrasting a higher intellectual activity with a lower, but a *feeling* which delights in the good and finds it sweet, with an intellectual activity.

Many examples could be given of this disjunction of knowledge and love: one must suffice. At the end of Sermon XXIII on the Song of Songs, Bernard considers three places where God reveals himself. In the first place, the soul sees God ordering the world. There the soul finds knowledge about God. It is a high and secret place, but not at all quiet (*altus et secretus, sed minime quietus*);[6] for the soul's desire for knowledge makes it restless. Here is contemplation, but here also is laborious searching. Here the bride says, 'I sleep, but my heart wakes'; 'for in sleep indeed she feels the repose of sweetest wonder and tranquil admiration, but she wakes, for she suffers the weariness of ceaseless curiosity and laborious effort.'[7] The next place is the place of the Judge. Here the soul is in fear because of her sins; here there is no rest. This second place, however, is more useful for the soul though apparently further from the bliss of rapture. For the first place was a place of merely intellectual contemplation, of knowledge; the second is a place where feeling is awakened, even though that feeling is fear. In the first place we learn; in the second we feel.

> *Instructio doctos reddit, affectio sapientes*: Instruction makes us learned, but feeling makes us wise ... Truly the fear of the Lord is the beginning of wisdom: we first taste God when he makes us fear him, not when he instructs us. You fear the righteousness of God, you fear his power; then you taste God, righteous and powerful, because fear is a sense of taste (*quia timor sapor est*).[8]

Beyond these two places where God is known there is a third place which is neither the lecture room of a professor nor the court of a judge: it is the bedchamber of the Bridegroom.

> O place of true quietness, which not unjustly is called the bedchamber ... That vision does not terrify, but soothes. It excites no restless curiosity, but stills it; nor does it weary the feeling but renders it tranquil. Here truly there is rest. God in his serenity makes everything serene; to behold such peace is to be peaceful oneself. (*Tranquillus Deus tranquillat omnia; et quietum aspicere, quiescere est*.)[9]

Bernard sums up his analogy thus:

> This is a bedchamber, and a bedchamber of the King, for of the three places, here alone is peace. In the first there is a little rest, in the second none at all. For in the first God is manifest as wonderful, which excites our curiosity; in the second as terrible, which crushes our weakness. In

the third place he is not terrible, nor even so much wonderful as lovable, serene and peaceful, sweet and gentle, and of great mercy to all who behold him.[10]

Sic affici, deificari est, we might think to ourselves, borrowing Bernard's own words. Here the soul *feels*; here the soul tastes the sweetness of God and is satisfied. But in this threefold vision (*triplex visio*, Bernard calls it), the soul passes from knowledge, through fear to love—the relation of the bride and the bridegroom. Knowledge is left behind because it does not involve feeling, and also because it dissipates the energy of the soul in a restless curiosity. Fear is valuable because it awakens feeling. Love is the soul's final state because the feeling of love totally absorbs the soul: 'When love comes, it draws everything else into itself and makes all feeling captive to itself.'[11]

Despite—or really because of—this disjunction of love and knowledge, Bernard's appreciation of the affective depths of the soul—depths only plumbed by love—gives him a conceptual tool which he handles with great skill in the exposition of his affective mysticism. Two examples will indicate what I mean. Both in his discussion of the relation of the soul to God, and its relation to other people, Bernard uses his appreciation of the feeling depths of the soul in a powerful way. Bernard is acutely aware of, and emphasizes, the particularity—even the uniqueness—of the relationship of each individual soul to God. 'For indeed there is not one queen only but several, and many concubines, and young women without number. And each finds a secret for herself with the Bridegroom, and says: My secret is mine, my secret is mine. (Isaiah 24:16).'[12]

An intellectual mysticism cannot but tend to detract from the uniqueness of the individual soul: the end is the vision of God, which is the same for all. And anyway, my knowledge is not mine but simply universal knowledge which I have apprehended. But my feelings are my own; and it is indeed with reference to the affective depths of the soul that Bernard explains the uniqueness of each soul's union with God. 'Now it is necessary that the relish of the divine presence should vary on account of the varying desires of the soul, and that the taste of heavenly sweetness should be felt on the soul's palate differently for each soul.'[13] The soul's palate—*animi palatum*, or *cordis palatum*. It is this that tastes the divine presence; and the flavour of such tasting is peculiar to each soul.

If his appreciation of affectivity enables Bernard to emphasize the uniqueness of each soul's experience of God, it also enables him to stress the community of one soul with another. The uniqueness of the soul's relation to God does not separate it from other souls. This comes out most clearly in his treatise *De Gradibus Humilitatis et Superbiae*. Here Bernard develops the idea that truth is apprehended in three ways: in ourselves, in others, and in itself. In ourselves, truth is attained by self-knowledge; in others, by compassion; in itself, by contemplation.

> Since there are therefore three grades or states of truth, we ascend to the first by the work of humility, to the second by the feeling of compassion, to the third by the transport of contemplation. In the first truth is discerned as severe, in the second as tender, in the third as pure. Reason leads us to the first, by which we examine ourselves; feeling draws us to the second, by which we have mercy on others; purity snatches us up to the third, by which we are raised to what is invisible.[14]

Two things are striking about this. First we have an ascent to mystical union with God which begins with self-knowledge (which is common enough) but which passes through an intermediate stage of compassion and love for other people. And secondly this intermediate stage is where our feeling is engaged. This mystic way requires introversion in one sense, but not in any way that withdraws us from other poeple. Far from it. It is in engagement with other people in love and compassion that we are prepared for union with God. The ascent begins in the school of humility. Those who have performed worthily there are introduced through their feeling, under the guidance of the Holy Spirit, into the *cellaria caritatis*, the chambers of love (a reference to Cant. 1:3) 'by which', Bernard remarks, 'doubtless are to be understood the hearts of our neighbours'.[15] Love of our neighbour, far from being something that might conflict with the love of God, is itself given a mystical dimension. Bernard's affective mysticism thus enables him to stress the community of souls one with another.

* * * * *

We have said that in Bernard and Augustine (and in Philo, in the mystical tradition of the Christian East, and indeed in Plato) we have a mysticism of love. But this can mean many things. Augustine's is a mysticism of desire for the knowledge of God. So too is Philo's, though with him love of God is brought into prominence because knowledge of God is impossible, God being unknowable. This linking of a mysticism of love with an apophatic doctrine of God is common in the East: God cannot be known, but he can be loved, and he will reveal himself to those who love him.

With Bernard we have something different from all this. God is not loved because he cannot be known. For, on the one hand, he can be known, though not in this life. Bernard is not ultimately apophatic, as Gregory of Nyssa is, for instance. And, on the other hand, if he could be known in this life it would not be desirable, for knowledge is distracting (it leads to curiosity). No, God is to be loved, according to Bernard, because it is only love that involves the whole man at his deepest. God is not to be sought as an object of knowledge, for knowledge does not affect man at all deeply—or not deeply enough, anyway. In *De Diligendo Deo*, Bernard considers the traditional three motives to be found in man's service of God: fear—the attitude of a slave; hope of reward—that of a labourer or mercenary; and love—the attitude of a son. Bernard is not unaware of the traditional line that fear and hope of reward make God a means for another end, but Bernard's point is different:

> There is love, which seeks not its own, in the son only. For this reason I think it is said of it: 'The law of the Lord is immaculate, converting souls.' For this alone, it seems, can turn the soul from love of self and the world and direct it to God. Neither fear nor the hope of reward can convert the soul; they may change one's manner, or even one's behaviour, but they can never touch one's feeling (*affectum*).... Love however converts souls by making them willing.[16]

Bernard's point is that only love *converts* the soul, effects a true *metanoia*, a true change at the deepest level. And it does this because it draws out one's will and one's feeling. 'Therefore he said: Learn of me, because I am meek and lowly of heart. Heart, he said, feeling of the heart, that is, the will.'[17] Bernard's mysticism of love is not based on his theology (or not entirely) as is Augustine's, for whom God is supremely desirable, namely, lovable; or Gregory of Nyssa's, for whom an unknowable God can yet be loved. Bernard's mysticism of love is based on his anthropology: God is to be loved, for in love man is most deeply engaged. Knowledge then will not do, for as a human activity it is superficial.

What Bernard gives us here is something new in the history of mystical theology. Bernard cannot be adequately appreciated if, with Abbot Butler, we regard him as simply an exponent of Augustinian, pre-Dionysian, western mysticism. Bernard's mysticism draws its power from his understanding of man's affective depths: only there is a man deeply engaged. Deep feeling is deeper than deep thought: and so a man's relationship to God—deep calling to deep—is a matter of feeling and not a matter of thought. It is true that Bernard relates knowledge and love as well as distinguishing them: 'What would be the effect of learning divorced from love? It would puff up. And of love divorced from learning? It would go astray.'[18] Yet this complementarity of knowledge and love is a wholly different matter from the apparently similar complementarity in Saint Augustine, say. There knowledge and love so coinhere that either without the other is inconceivable. This coinherence clearly affects our understanding of both knowledge and love. Mere ratiocination and simple emotion are clearly different: but then the former is not true knowledge, nor is the latter genuine love. True knowledge and genuine love coincide—in *sapientia*. With Bernard, however, they are different and remain distinct. They are complementary, as our quotation above shows; but what that means is that knowledge by itself is bad for man, and love without knowledge might find itself directed towards the wrong object. Love would still engage the whole man (at least potentially); but so much the worse, for unless our mind tells us that only God is to be loved for himself alone, we might pour out our love worthlessly. True knowledge and real love do not coincide for Bernard: they are complementary, but quite distinct.

In his disjunction between thought and feeling, Bernard is very modern. We are moved by our feelings, not by our thoughts: feeling is, in that sense, deeper than thought. Augustine, in contrast, does not make or feel such a disjunction, and in that he is at one with Plato (and Plotinus) who finds the heights and depths of man in his intelligence (not indeed in his capacity for discursive thought, but in something more intuitive). Plato was a mathematician, and placed great emphasis on the importance of mathematics in the training of the soul. Perhaps a mathematician can more easily understand how pure thought can move, that thought and feeling are not separate, still less thought a mere handmaid of feeling.

What these reflections suggest—at least to the writer of them—is that in Bernard we have a shift in the understanding of man, a shift that renders no longer tenable the classical, Platonic-Augustinian synthesis. 'The new thing itself, I do not pretend to explain. Real changes in human sentiment are very rare—there are perhaps three or four on record—but I believe they do occur, and that this is one of them.'[19] C.S. Lewis said that of the emergence of the ideal of courtly love; one is tempted to echo his remark apropos Bernard's mysticism. A shift in the understanding of the roots of human thought and feeling; and the desertion of the Platonic-Augustinian synthesis. Perhaps in this more of the truth is brought within man's compass; nevertheless something of the truth becomes inaccessible. Thought is separated from feeling, theology from spirituality. Alone they may bear more splendid fruits; but we miss the fruit they once bore together.

* * * * *

NOTES

All references to the works of St. Bernard are given to the treatise (by name—or sermon by number) and section, and also by volume, page, and line reference in the definitive edition by Dom J. Leclercq and others (*S. Bernardi Opera*, Romae, Editiones Cistercienses, 1957- . VII volumes so far).

1. 'The Influence of Pseudo-Dionysius on Western Mysticism' in *Christian Spirituality*. Essays in honour of Gordon Rupp. Edited by Peter Brooks. SCM Press, 1975, pp. 79ff.

2. *De Diligendo Deo* X.27; III, 142, 9-12.

3. Ibid.; III, 143, 15.

4. Ibid. VIII.23; III, 138, 6.

5. See *In Cant. Sermo* 85; II, 312f.

6. *In Cant. Sermo* 23, IV.11; I, 145, 28.

7. Ibid.; I, 146, 6-9.

8. Ibid. V.14; I, 147, 24 and 148, 4-7.

9. Ibid. VI.16; I, 149, 16f. and 19-21.

10. Ibid.; I, 150, 3-10 (somewhat condensed).

11. *In Cant. Sermo* 83.I.3; II, 300, 3f.

12. Ibid. 23.IV.9; I, 144, 29-31.

13. Ibid. 31.III.7; I, 223, 22-24.

14. Op. cit. VI.19; III, 30, 28-31, 5.

15. Ibid. VII.21; III, 32, 24f.

16. *De Diligendo Deo* XII.34; III, 148, 20-149, 4 and 149, 11f.

17. *In Cant. Sermo* 42.IV.7; II, 37, 23-25.

18. Ibid. 69.II.2; II, 203, 4f.

19. C.S. Lewis: *The Allegory of Love*, O.U.P. 1936, p. 11.

CONTEMPLATION AND ACTION IN THE PASTORAL THEOLOGY OF ST. BERNARD

Martin Smith, SSJE

AN IMPORTANT THEME in the writings of Bernard of Clairvaux is the relation between the contemplative and active dimensions of Christianity. He has a great deal to say about how this is experienced within the monastic life, especially by those who occupy a pastoral role within the monastic community. Not only does he reflect deeply in his sermons both about the tension he experienced between his call to mystical prayer and his teaching office as abbot, and also their mutual interdependence and fruitfulness; he had to endure as well the most extreme tension between his monastic vocation as such and the demands of the intense political and spiritual action in the Church at large to which the crises of his age called him. And of this his letters speak with candour and pain. For St Bernard, the active and contemplative lives are not in conflict or rivalry with each other. The society of the Church is divided into distinct *ordines* with separate responsibilities; the monastic order with its contemplative orientation complements the others with their equally vital active roles. He expresses this differentiation of responsibilities amongst Christian vocations and the *'concatenatio'*, or bond which unites them in amusing symbolism. For instance, he calls the monastic order the Church's teeth or stomach. In an interpretation of the various categories of people involved in the events of Palm Sunday, he compares it with the ass on which the Lord was carried: the point is that the monk's role is highly privileged, though an unspectacular one to which not much attention is given. Monks 'are the ones who have chosen an excellent part: living for God alone, in the cloister, they are always united to Him and they think only of what will please Him. . . . Those who are thus united to Him are the contemplatives' (Sermon II, *'In Ramis Palmarum'*).

Consequently, conflict does occur when circumstances force a mature member of one *'ordo'* to leave it for another. A more dramatic example could scarcely be imagined than that of the election as Pope in 1145 of Eugenius, the Cistercian Abbot of St. Anastasius, a former monk of Clairvaux. Although Bernard could not suppress a certain gratification which he revealed to the new Pope, he also expressed a sense of outrage at the unnaturalness of this translation when he wrote to the Curia: 'God have mercy on you; what have you done?' He demands the reason for choosing a 'dead man ... crucified to the world ... a beggar, a penitent, a rustic' to occupy the Papal throne with its dangerous risks and responsibilities. He asks them to imagine 'the feelings of a man who from the secrets of contemplation and the sweet solitude of his heart suddenly finds himself plunged into a vortex of great affairs like a child snatched from his mother's arms' (letter 315). This total transformation of role required an entirely new spiritual orientation which Bernard set out to provide in his special treatise of Papal pastoral theology, *'De Consideratione'*. In particular, the tension between contemplation and action takes on for the new Pope a different form. It is no longer a matter of seeking, within an environment designed to facilitate contemplation, the correct balance of solitary repose with pastoral charity. It is now a question of ensuring, within the turmoil of the Court and the crushing demands of the Papacy, adequate attention to *'consideratio'*, by which is meant an all-embracing, keen reflectiveness (which merges into contemplation when divine things are its subject).

Bernard begins by commiserating with Eugenius: 'If I am not mistaken, you are reluctantly torn from the embraces of your Rachel and as often as that befalls you your sorrow must be renewed. But when does that not happen?' (Book 1, ch. 1), and he warns him that if he gets hardened to ceaseless activity his spiritual life will be irreparable damaged. Bernard presents several arguments to support the priority of *'consideratio'*. First, without it the Pope's activities themselves will be unavailing and unprofitable. *'Consideratio'* 'by a kindly anticipation' creates 'the divisions of the active life itself, in a manner rehearsing and arranging beforehand what has to be done. ... [It] purifies the very fountain, that is the mind, from which it springs. Then it governs the affections, directs our actions, corrects excesses, softens the manners, adorns and regulates the life, and, lastly, bestows the knowledge of things divine and human alike. It is *"consideratio"* that brings order out of disorder, puts in the links, pulls things together, investigates mysteries, traces the truth, weighs probabilities, exposes shams and counterfeits' (Book 1, ch. 7).

His second argument has an interestingly modern appeal. Bernard praises the attitude which says that he now belongs altogether to other people, but cleverly renders it useless as a justification for activism. 'I praise your humanity but only on condition that it be complete. But how can it be complete if you yourself are left out? You too are a man. So then, in order that your humanity may be entire and complete, let your bosom, which receives all, find room for yourself also.' That is, to provide time for meditation and solitude is a pastoral duty towards oneself; failure in this mars one's whole ministry. 'In short if a man is bad to himself, to whom is he good? So remember, I do not say always, I do not say often, but at least sometimes, to restore yourself to yourself' (Book 1, ch. 5).

Thirdly, Bernard implies that the contemplative orientation he is recommending, by demanding time, has the excellent reforming effect of forcing the Pope to prune his activities ruthlessly; he will have to refuse to preside over superfluous litigation, the endless appeals to the Holy See which had been such a disastrous feature of previous reigns and he will have to delegate most of the material administration of the Papal household. Finally, Bernard presents in the last book an analysis of the stages of *consideratio* particularly useful for someone living in the world. ' *"Consideratio"* is "economical"—that of the steward—when it makes systematic use of the senses and of sensible things in daily life so as to win the favour of God. It is "estimative"—that of the valuer—when it wisely and diligently searches everything and weighs everything to find God. It is "speculative" when it retires within itself, and, so far as Divine help is given, detaches itself from human affairs in order to contemplate God' (Book 5, ch. 2).

These pastoral directives towards a new spiritual orientation for Eugenius are remarkably coherent. But with regard to his own case things were more difficult. Bernard found it impossible to give a really cogent rationale for his own highly ambiguous existence. He could not claim to have been definitively drawn in this way from one sphere to another. He was trying to live the life of monastic solitude and public action and had to admit that the attempt was a weird anomaly. It is understandable that he should be most conscious of this when writing to Carthusians, maintaining their solitude in integrity. He finishes the letter on this note of rueful self-mockery: 'It is time for me to remember myself. May my monstrous life, my bitter conscience move you to pity. I am a sort of modern chimaera, neither cleric nor layman. I have kept the habit of a monk but I have long ago abandoned the life. I do not wish to tell you what I dare say you have heard from others; what I am doing, what are my purposes, through what dangers I pass in the world, or rather down what precipices I am hurled' (Letter 326). A chimaera was a hybrid monster of Greek mythology: lion before, she-goat in the middle, and serpent behind!

It would take too long to re-tell the story of how a career which began in chosen solitude was drawn outwards to influence successively wider spheres until Bernard became one of the key figures of Christendom whose power could be felt from Scotland to Jerusalem. His activites began with preaching expeditions in the neighbourhood of Clairvaux. Soon were added the arduous journeys and labours in making new Cistercian foundations—no less than sixty-five were made from Clairvaux alone by the time of his death in 1153. He rapidly gained such a reputation amongst the hierarchy and other religious orders as a conciliator and consultant that his enormous correspondence came to require the labours of two secretaries. He was pressed into writing a wide variety of tracts and books. His travelling intensified particularly after the Council of Étampes (1130) as he went back and forth tirelessly championing Innocent II against the antipope Anacletus. In 1135 he took part in the Diet of Bamberg and then made his way to Italy to appease the rebels at Milan. He returned to Italy in 1137. In 1140 we find him in Paris and then at the Council of Sens for the condemnation of Abelard. In 1145 he journeyed to Languedoc in the campaign against the Henrician heretics, and the two years following the preaching of the Second Crusade at Vézelay in 1146 saw him incessantly on the road trying to get the armies on the move. In 1148 we see him at Rheims pressing the condemnation of Gilbert de la Porée, and in the very year of his death he went on a peace-making expedition to Lorraine.

His repeated protests against the attempts of others to involve him in the wider affairs of the Church are due neither to mere modesty, let alone false modesty, nor to a conventional wish to play safe by 'sticking to his corner'. Rather they are a defence of God's absolute right to call whom He will to monastic solitude, even those with talents which seem to make them eligible as ecclesiastical statesmen. 'If these matters in which you try to involve your friend at the cost of his peace and silence are simple, then they can be settled without me; if they are difficult then they cannot be settled by me. Unless I am considered a person of such consequence that great and difficult matters must be reserved for me because there is no one else to settle them. If this is so then only in my case have the designs of God been frustrated. Why has He put me under a bushel when I could give light from a candlestick, or, to speak more clearly, why, if I am necessary to the world, a man without whose aid the bishops cannot settle their own affairs, has God called me to be a monk and "hidden me in his tabernacle in the day of evil things"?' (Letter 22.) 'Not teaching but lamenting is the duty of the monk I am supposed to be and the sinner that I am' (letter 92). These misgivings of his own were reinforced by the sharp criticism he had to bear for his interference, from his eminent friend Cardinal Haimeric for instance.

The force which outweighed these misgivings was, to quote the early biography of the saint, his 'greatest desire . . . the salvation of all mankind . . . the great passion of his heart from the first day of his life as a monk even to the day on which I am writing this' (*Vita Prima*, ch. 10). Paradoxically, it was this burning universal care for the Church which Bernard taught was the essence of monastic intercession and ascetical vigilance which reached such an intensity in himself that it caused him to cross what he, as well as other, recognized to be the proper limits of monastic action. This concern for the Church is consistently theocentric. So an uncertain matter of a deputation from Rheims to the Holy See engages him not as a political affair but a Divine one. 'I will be importunate, but it will be the importunity of charity, truth and justice. Although I am not so important as to have affairs at Rome, yet nothing that concerns the glory of God is a matter of indifference to me' (letter 21). It was a concern especially alive to the supreme priority of the Church's unity. He felt justified in his own activities and his unrelenting efforts to mobilise others to action, by his conviction that schism in particular was utterly critical. 'Can you sit by while your mother the Church is troubled? There has been a time of rest. Holy leisure has hitherto exercised its arts freely and lawfully. Now is the time for action, because the law has been broken' (letter 128).

He insists that his concern was never translated into action except under obedience. He transgressed the bounds of what is proper to the monastic state only when insistently urged to do so by the Church's authorities. He always leaves his monastery under duress, his reluctance undiminished by the increasing frequency of the demands caused by his astonishing success; but as soon as the act of obedience had been made, then all the fervour distilled in his solitude and all the intensity of his 'great passion' was focussed on the action in question. The duress under which he entered the arena of action caused him neither to drag his feet nor to justify himself with a hybrid 'mixed life' theory which sought a compromise between solitude and engagement. Everything he had and was he threw into the action.

We now turn to St. Bernard's treatment of the polarity of contemplation and action within monastic life itself. He stands of course in the mainstream of patristic and monastic tradition. In this, the 'active life' refers to the Christian's effort to acquire the virtues by means of the habitual practice of charity towards his neighbours and also by the disciplines of personal asceticism. The active life is not only the indispensible stage through which one must pass in order to aspire to contemplative prayer, but it is also a lifelong commitment upon which the contemplative must re-engage himself between the inevitably fleeting experiences of contemplation. The harmonious organic relationship between action and contemplation understood in this way, will give way to disorder and tension when a monk attempts to take a short cut to contemplation on the one hand, or on the other tries to prolong self-indulgently the privileged repose of contemplation.

Bernard warns against the first error in sermon 46 on the Song of Songs. (All succeeding quotations will be from this series unless otherwise noted.) 'Therefore take care ... to make the exercise of the virtues precede that holy leisure. Otherwise it would be self-indulgence that you should so earnestly desire to rest before you have earned that rest by labour, and you would be neglecting the fruitfulness of Lia in desiring to enjoy only the embraces of Rachel. ... Do not imagine then that love of your own repose is to be made a hindrance to works of holy obedience, or to the traditions of the elders. Do not suppose that you will have the company of the Bridegroom for that bed which you have strewed not with the flowers of obedience but with the weeds and nettles of disobedience.' Bernard teaches in the next sermon that the reward of contemplation is intrinsically related to the work which 'earns' it. 'The good actions of a holy life are well compared to the flowers in a bridal chamber because they produce the testimony of a quiet and safe conscience. After a good work one more securely reposes in contemplation; and the more fully a man is conscious of not having been wanting through inertness or love of self in the performance of good works the more confidence he will have in endeavouring to see and to investigate things on high.'

He warns against the second error of trying to linger in contemplative repose in Sermon 51. He insists that the actual experiences of contemplation are of necessity fleeting. Whenever 'the light of contemplation is withdrawn from [the soul] as is often the case', there is spiritual and moral danger if he does not return at once to good works. 'As often as he falls from the state of contemplation he resorts to that of action as to a convenient refuge from whence he may be able more easily to return into contemplation. For these two things are intimately related; they are chamber companions and dwell together. Martha is sister to Mary and although she comes forth from the light of contemplation she never suffers herself to fall into the darkness of sin or subside into slothful leisure but remains still in the light of good works.' The reference to Martha and Mary, and also to Lia and Rachel, as representative of the active and contemplative life derives, of course, through St. Gregory the Great from St. Augustine.

The problem of doing justice to both dimensions of Christian life was felt most acutely by the monastic pastors and officials, subject as they were to the pressures of time-consuming business and the never-ending spiritual needs of what were often immense communities. First there was the danger that a monk might actually 'aspire to the tumultuous life of the officials'; St. Bernard warns against that snare in the third sermon on the Assumption, presumably because, as he observes elsewhere, it was often the case that it was 'an impatient and restless disposition' which kept people in office. Nevertheless, when a monk was appointed to some official position it could be the opportunity for that heroic self-sacrifice which consisted in shouldering the burdens of administration so completely (however much that went against the grain of his own longing for contemplation), that at the cost of his own leisure, others were enabled to have solitude, peace and the opportunity to instruct the brethren. This was the costly vocation of Bernard's brother Gerard who was cellarer of Clairvaux. Bernard paid him moving tribute for it in Sermon 26 on the Song of Songs.

Pastoral responsibility of a spiritual kind was held not only by the abbot and prior but also by 'spiritual brethren'. It was excercised apparently not in formal classes or conferences—there is hardly a sign of systematic and collective novitiate training for instance—but primarily through 'confession'. This was not the same as the sacrament of penance as now understood but was the traditional practice of personal spiritual counselling in private interviews. In these the monk would seek guidance and encouragement by opening his heart and revealing his current spiritual condition, 'confessing' his experiences, whether they were ones of aridity and temptation or of consolation and progress. In order to reduce the pressure on these pastors and allow them to pursue the contemplative life, everyone in the community has to practice restraint in availing himself of their ministry. Everyone has to take to heart the warning, 'I charge you, O ye daughters of Jerusalem, by the roes and hinds of the field, that ye stir not up nor wake my love till she pleases.' But, as Bernard acknowledges in Sermon 52, it was difficult to sound that warning without having the distressing effect of discouraging the timid from revealing their spiritual needs to him and seeking his help. However, when this restraint is practised widely with discretion it can be regarded as a strong sign of God's favour for the contemplative. 'The Bride, noticing the increased modesty of her maidens and their respectful timidity shewn by their no longer venturing to intrude upon her sacred repose, nor presuming as they had previously done, to trouble the quiet of her contemplation, recognises that this is the effect of the care and labours of the Bridegroom. Rejoicing therefore in spirit as well because they are advantaged in being restrained from needless and excessive restlessness as because of the condescension and favour of her Bridegroom and her own prospect of unbroken quiet in future she declares that it is the voice of her Beloved which does this . . .' (Sermon 53).

In this passage Bernard shews a strong sense that it is God Himself who resolves the conflicting claims of action and contemplation; His providence is at work not only in His direct relationship with the contemplative pastor himself but also in the entire community to create the conditions in which the needs of the pastor and the brethren can be equally met, This divine initiative also decrees the times for active ministry as much as the times for withdrawal. And again this is no mere alternation of occupations. Rather, pastoral zeal and fervour come to maturity as the natural outcome of mystical prayer. 'After this divine look, so full of condescension and goodness, comes a voice gently and sweetly presenting to the mind the Will of God; and this is no other than Love itself, which cannot remain in leisure, soliciting and persuading to the fulfilment of the things that are of God. Thus the Bride hears that she is to arise and hasten, no doubt to work for the good of souls. This is indeed a property of true and pure contemplation, that it sometimes fills the mind, which it has vehemently inflamed with divine fire, with a fervent zeal and desire to gain for God others to love Him in like manner and to that end willingly lays aside the leisure of contemplation for the labour of preaching.' In turn, the effectiveness of work done as the outcome of prayer acts as stimulus to return to contemplation. 'And again when it has attained the object desired, to a certain extent, it returns with the more eagerness to that contemplation, in that it remembers that it laid it aside for the sake of more fruit' (Sermon 57).

However, this guidance cannot be taken for granted and it does not always make itself obvious. The monastic pastor has to accept as part of his vocation a state of anxiety. Bernard does not idealize his situation or speak glibly about the harmony between action and contemplation but writes realistically about his constant state of psychological suspense and misgiving. 'But the mind frequently hesitates between these continual changes, being profoundly anxious and fearful, lest when drawn to one or other of these alternatives by the attractions and advantages it discerns in each, it should give itself up too much to one or other of them and should deviate ever so little from the divine will . . . Even a holy man feels grave uncertainty between the claims of fruitful labour and restful contemplation; and although he is always occupied about good things, yet he always feels a sense of regret as if he had been doing that which is wrong and from one moment to another retreats with groans to be shewn the will of God. In these uncertainties the one and only remedy is prayer and frequent uplifting of the soul to God, that he would deign to make continually known to us what we ought to do, and when, how, and in what manner we should do it' (Sermon 57).

Contemplation, then, in a general way, fills one with love and zeal for pastoral action; but it is particularly intimately related to one form of that ministry—namely that of preaching—because in contemplation God imparts knowledge in the deepest and fullest sense of the word. In Book 2, chapter 2 of the treatise 'On Consideration', Bernard had indicated the epistemological value of contemplation in this way. 'Contemplation may be defined as the true and certain intuition of any object, or the certain apprehension of truth.' His twenty-third sermon on the Song of Songs describes how the soul is initiated by Contemplation into understanding God's rule over His creatures, His justice and His mercy. The knowledge gained in mystical experience is far removed from intellectual information and is effective on emotional and volitional levels deeper than the intellect. 'It is in truth "the Spirit of wisdom and understanding" Who, like the bee bearing wax and honey, has wherewith to light the lamp of knowledge and the warmth of love' (Sermon 8). It is only to his friends and lovers God communicates His secrets, for to them alone was it said, 'All things whatsoever I have heard of my Father I have made known to you'. Indeed, as the blessed Gregory teaches, love not only merits but is itself this knowledge' (Sermon 29 of the series, *'de diversis'*).

Consequently, the need to preach responsibly is a motive for the more ardent pursuit of contemplation, because only in prayer can the monastic pastor equip himself to teach his flock. St. Bernard warns against the danger of embarking on the ministry of preaching prematurely, out of hasty ambition. 'Why do you not wait for the light? Why do you presume to undertake the work of light before the light is with you? It is vain to rise before the light dawns upon you' (Sermon 62). Furthermore, it is a temptation to begin to impart teaching to others before one is endowed fully; the danger here is of draining oneself and damaging one's own inner life by too ready a release of what one has been given so far. The other risk is that of cheating others by faulty and immature teaching. 'You lose and dissipate that which is your own, if, before you have receive a complete inpouring, and while you are, so to speak, but half-filled, you hasten to pour yourself forth. . . . If then you are wise you will shew yourself rather as a reservoir than as a canal. For a canal spreads abroad water as it receives it, but a reservoir waits until it is filled before overflowing and thus communicates, without loss to itself, its superabundant water. In the Church at the present day we have many canals, few reservoirs' (Sermon 18). In the same sermon Bernard warns against the contrary danger of 'a useless or rather blameable silence' prompted by fear, sloth or ill-judged humility in men with gifts of knowledge and eloquence. There is as much danger of keeping for ourselves what is given to us for others as of giving to others what is meant for ourselves.

The welling up in the soul of this mystical knowledge, so distinct from worldly learning, is in fact evidence that the mystical embrace has been given; the experience itself is ineffable, indescribable, but if fills the soul with a new ability to nourish those under its care. Bernard uses the vivid erotic/maternal imagery provided by the Song of Songs like this: 'And the Bridegroom will say: Thou hast, O my spouse, that which thou prayedst for; and this is the sign—thy breasts have become more precious than wine. Thence shalt thou know that thou hast received [the embrace] because thou hast become fruitful. Therefore have thy breasts filled with abundance of milk better than the wine of wordly knowledge which inebriates indeed but with curiosity not charity, which fills but does not nourish; which puffs up instead of edifying, which gluts but strengthens not' (Sermon 9).

It was by developing the imagery of spiritual marriage, the great theme of the Sermons on the Song of Songs, to include that of spiritual fecundity that Bernard was able to express his 'last word' on the subject of the reconciliation of the call to prayer and the call to service in the life of the monastic pastor. Fittingly enough the sermon which expresses it best was almost literally his last word; his death cut short the one that followed it. 'When you shall see a soul which, having left all, cleaves unto the Word with every thought and desire; lives only for the Word, rules itself according to the Word, nay, becomes fruitful by the Word—which is able to say 'To me to live is Christ and to die is gain'; then you may have assurance that this soul is a bride wedded to the Word.' The consummation of mystical union gives rise to two sorts of motherhood. The primary one is a giving birth to 'spiritual intellections' by meditation, arising from the intimate presence of the Word Himself. The other is the motherhood which brings forth souls by preaching. So Bernard traces back both elements in the monastic pastor's life, the contemplative and the active, and shews how they have an identical origin and turn on a common axis—the spiritual union which the monk continually seeks. In the imagery of spiritual marriage and motherhood he is able to express how, in the end, the mystical quest is the true mainspring of the monastic pastor's life, and at the same time do justice to the satisfying joyfulness and importance of his ministry. 'Indeed a mother has joy in her offspring, but a bride has greater joy in the embraces of her spouse. Dear are children, the pledges of affection, but kisses give greater joy. It is a great work to save many souls, but to be transported and to be with the Word, that is far more delightful. But when does that happen, and how long does it endure? Sweet is that intercourse; but how seldom does it occur and for how brief a time does it last. And this is the final reason for which the soul seeks the Word; namely that it may find delight through enjoying Him.' (Sermon 85.)

Sources of extracts from the works of St. Bernard:

Saint Bernard - On Consideration, tr. by George Lewis, Oxford 1908.

Life and Works of St. Bernard, vol. 4, tr. by Samuel J. Eales, London 1896.

Western Mysticism, Cuthbert Butler, 2nd ed., London 1926.

The Letters of St. Bernard of Clairvaux, tr. by Bruno Scott James, London 1953.

THREE STYLES OF MONASTIC REFORM

Rowan Williams

IT IS A COMMON ENOUGH ERROR in considering Saint Bernard and the early Cistercians to view them in a somewhat restricted and foreshortened perspective; to adopt, consciously or unconsciously, the popular view of the Cistercians as the climacteric and most successful representatives of a general movement in the eleventh and twelfth centuries of reaction against a corrupt and more or less lax and 'secularized' Benedictinism, towards primitive purity of monastic observance. My purpose in this essay is to attempt some modifications of this picture; although I have neither the desire nor the competence to question the indebtedness of many early Cistercian writers to the Greek Fathers and the ideals of desert monasticism,[1] I believe that it is important to recognize what it was that distinguished the Cistercians from other monastic radicals and 'primitivists'— what it was, in fact, that made them so much more successful in their day than other reforming bodies, why they spoke so much more clearly and influentially to the secular world of the twelfth century than did the Camaldolesi or the Carthusians. This is a question of more than merely historical interest: the ideals of monastic reformers change surprisingly little from age to age, and the theorists of monastic renewal at the present time may have a good deal to learn from a study of 'styles of reform' in earlier ages, in both their weak and their strong points. With this in mind, I shall first go back beyond the twelfth century to the first great wave of reforming activity beginning in the Carolingian period, around 800, and culminating in the foundation of Cluny and its establishment as the focus of an international 'new monasticism',[2] in order to consider briefly what we may call the 'ideology' of the reformers—what they thought they were doing—as a necessary preliminary for the understanding of the later reforms.

I

As Knowles[3] has pointed out, European monasticism 'between the death of St. Gregory and the age of Charlemagne' was anything but a homogeneous institution. The Rule of St. Benedict was, for a long time and in many areas, one among a large and diverse assortment of rules, some of them connected with a particular 'master' such as Columbanus, others virtual anthologies of classical ascetic texts;[4] and although some kind of practical consensus in observance had been reached by the end of the eighth century, this was a mixture of widely differing elements, and constituted a way of life markedly unlike that envisaged directly by Benedict. The Rule—it must be stated firmly—was in no way understood as law or as constitution: the community is, if we may so express it, prior to the Rule, which is seen as ordering and guiding in a general way a communal life growing out of the tradition of particular houses. What was achieved by the Carolingian reforms associated with the name of Benedict of Aniane was a recognition of the Rule of St. Benedict as an official point of reference, as *the* rule; although observance continued to diverge from the letter of the Rule, it was nonetheless true from this time on that the final court of appeal for the greater part of Western European monasticism was to be St. Benedict's Rule and no other. In fact, the *Capitula* of Aachen, which, in 817, imposed these reforms by law on the Carolingian Empire, established a type of observance which was to set the standard for 'black' Benedictinism throughout the Middle Ages—and, indeed, to the present day. The *Capitula* imposed not merely the Rule, but the agreed interpretations and alterations of Benedict of Aniane and his circle.[5] The most significant modifications were the drastic reduction of the agricultural labour to be undertaken by monks and the considerable increase in the quantity of obligatory public prayer and psalmody: St. Benedict had envisaged his communities as self-supporting families, engaged in subsistence farming balanced by private reading and communal psalmody; Benedict of Aniane comes near to *defining* the monk as a professional executant of liturgy.

Obviously, Benedict of Aniane does not bear sole responsibility for this shift of emphasis: the influence of practice in the great basilican monasteries of Rome, of the usages of Celtic monachism, and (a subject that could do with further study) perhaps of the reformed Byzantine model established by Theodore of Studium, all contributed to it. However, it was his energy and ability which, in the words of H.B.de Warren,[6] 'guaranteed as complete a triumph as possible for the Benedictine Rule, without constantly laying claim to an observance as literal . . . as the Cistercians were to carry out'. If we ask how the Rule was viewed in this context, the answer is that it was inextricably linked with 'custom', the tradition not primarily of the house but of the Carolingian *Capitula*: monastic 'law' is the Rule as understood at Aachen and as modified by Benedict of Aniane.[7] The Rule is not *in itself* law; it is, rather, a document of primary historical and spiritual importance, a 'definition of an ethos', enshrined within the practical prescriptions of law, but not itself constituting those prescriptions exclusively, exhaustively or unalterably. The place it occupies in monastic life is far closer to that taken by the 'Rules' of Basil in Eastern monasticism, or by the 'Rule' of Augustine in the later constitutions of the Dominican Order, than to that which it came to occupy in much mediaeval and post-mediaeval Benedictinism.

The foundation and organization of Cluny and its dependencies in the tenth century represented a movement towards a more unified and strict monastic observance after the disastrous decline of reformed Benedictinism which followed the breaking up of the Carolingian Empire; but it was, as has already been implied, essentially a *continuation* of the Carolingian reform, sharing its general understanding of rule and custom. The great Odo of Cluny, in a sermon on St. Benedict, compares the saint with Moses, not (as we might expect) as a solitary legislator of unique authority, but as a uniquely great *codifier* and organizer of a large body of traditional material;[8] a judgment which, for its age, exhibits an unusually sophisticated historical sense. The Rule for Odo and his followers remains a supremely useful digest of monastic *theology*; it has not become a self-sufficient 'code'. Thus the monastic community envisaged by the Cluniac reformers is, to an even greater extent than the model presupposed in the Aachen *Capitula*, a social phenomenon quite significantly different from that for which the first Benedict had written, though claiming a real continuity with this latter, and looking to Benedict as its inspirer and (in a loose sense) director. And the major difference, as Knowles rightly says,[9] was that Cluny understood the monastic life as *essentially* liturgical—liturgical, that is, as opposed to contemplative (*stricto sensu*), or scholarly, or agrarian, or missionary (though none of these elements was ever wholly absent, except perhaps the agrarian)—thus developing to their logical conclusion the principles of the Carolingian Reform. However, more must be said: it is important to understand precisely what 'liturgical' means in this context. The 'work of God' in Benedict's Rule is simply and exclusively the prayer performed by the community as a community; but by the tenth century it can no longer be defined simply in these terms. It has become 'social', public, a work of intercession on behalf of society. In the words of Odo himself,[10] the job of the monk is the 'accumulation' or 'gaining' (*lucrum*) of souls by their devoutness and their works of charity. And this, of course, applies equally to souls in purgatory: Cluny under its fifth abbot, Odilo, established the observance of All Souls' Day,[11] with a very full liturgical round. Outside the directly Cluniac world, the English monasteries connected with Dunstan's reforms and the *Regularis Concordia* of 943 pushed the 'social' reference of liturgy to a unique degree, with an extraordinary proliferation of special prayers for the royal house.[12]

Cluniac monasticism, for all its sincere profession of *contemptus mundi*, its ascetical and even eschatological concerns,[13] gave the monastery a clearly defined social function and location: not only was it the place where prayer was offered for the rest of society, it was also the upholder of certain social values in a world which sat rather light to them. The almost obsessive concern with peace, whether between local magnates or between Empire and Papacy, which sent Odo and his successors on their constant and laborious journeys,[14] produced some surprising concrete results in the shape of 'God's Truce' in the eleventh century, short-lived and precarious as this arrangement was.[15] And open-handed charity to the poor was from the beginning a noted characteristic of Cluny (even in the days before it had accumulated the great wealth of its 'golden age').[16] Without entering into the vexed and continuing debate over Cluny's exact connexion with the reforms of Gregory VII, it is perfectly clear that Cluniac influence was of great importance in the general reforming movement in the tenth and eleventh centuries.[17] In short, Cluny was a social and political phenomenon of enormous significance, an energetic, powerful and apparently tireless force in Church and society, pressing both towards a stricter allegiance to the values of the gospel as understood in the monastic world—harmony, charity, and integrity. It is essential to recognize, as Morghen reminds us,[18] that Cluny in its early days was *not* concerned with 'involvement in affairs' and political or social influence as such; it understood its mission as a protest against the 'secularisation' of Christian authority by a corrupt clerisy, against accomodation to the world (hence, Morghen points out, the marked eschatological interests of Odo). But the familiar paradox rapidly asserted itself: a reform understood as reaction to certain aspects of Church or society is *defined* by what it reacts against, and so, finally, cannot escape from society. It comes to occupy a place *within* society—even if it is, as it were, marked with a negative sign: the unworldly is domesticated into the world, into a special 'sacral' area of society, and its protest is thereby neutralized. What is more, the way is thus opened for a return to 'accomodation', secularization. It is a vicious circle, a sterile dialectic, repeated again and again in Christian history—the Constantinian Church, the Gregorian Reform, the polity of Calvin, British Nonconformist Liberalism—and Cluny was one of its most notable victims.

II

The legalization of Christianity by Constantine, and the beginnings of an essay in theocracy in the fourth-century Empire were among the complex and obscure factors which prompted the rise of the monastic movement in that period:[19] martyrdom was no longer a possibility, the eschatological tension between Church and society was obscured by the ideologists of the Christian Empire, and a form of radical protest became necessary. So in the eleventh century we find a pervasive sense that Cluny and the Gregorian Reform, and all they represented, were an inadequate response to the compromised state of Christendom: 'reformism' was not enough. Peter Damian, the most prominent 'radical' of the century, looks back quite explicity to the pre-Constantinian church as a model in his reforming activity: in a celebrated passage in one of his sermons,[20] he exhorts his congregation to 'go back . . . to the innocence of the primitive Church, so that we may learn both to abandon our possessions and to rejoice in the simplicity of the royal estate of poverty'. Elsewhere, in a letter,[21] Damian (very significantly) argues that the fact that the age of martyrdom, the age of the Church's 'struggle', is over does not mean that the attitudes associated with martyrdom are obsolete: the Church in its 'peace-time' must preserve the same discipline which produced the martyrs, must maintain absolute detachment from the world at the heart of its life by the practice of the most rigorous asceticism. In common with several patristic writers, Damian takes Philo's *'De Vita Contemplativa'* to be evidence for the existence of Christian 'monks' in Egypt in the first century A.D.; and indeed, he goes so far as to say that the ascetics described by Philo are simply Christians in general, not a special class among them[22]—that is to say, that monastic asceticism is identical with Christian life as it should be lived. In contrast to the presupposition of Cluniac monasticism, that the monk is a functionary in Church and society, Damian sees monastic withdrawal—and especially monastic poverty—as the essential mark of the Christian, *toutcourt*: the monk is not (to adapt the famous phrase of Eric Gill about men and artists) a special kind of Christian; every Christian is a special kind of monk.

It would be absurd to press this distinction too far, or even to claim that it was (or could have been) plainly articulated by either side. Damian admired Cluny (though not unreservedly), was on friendly terms with the great Abbot Hugh, and, at the latter's prompting, wrote the life of Abbot Odilo; and in terms of practical politics his position had a good deal in common with that favoured by Cluny, aiming at a careful balance of power between Empire and Papacy. Damian is one of the first theologians actually to make explicit the distinction of *sacerdotium* from *regnum*, and to use the image of the 'two swords' to describe the parallel authorities of the Pope and the Emperor. But it is most important to recognize that, even in this context, Damian insists most vehemently that ecclesiastical authority is different in *kind* from worldly authority: violent coercion is totally alien to the Christian conception of authority, and the Church betrays itself if it adopts the machinery of secular power.[23] The Christian ideal, once again, is to be understood in terms of what were considered in that age to be characteristically 'monastic' virtues, humility, obedience and service.

Damian's attitude to specifically monastic reform is, as we might expect, correspondingly strict, based upon the purity of primitive models. He had himself been a monk of the house of Santa Croce at Fonte Avellana, a monastery which followed the observance of the Benedictine Rule devised by Romuald, the great reformer of the early years of the eleventh century. Romuald's interpretation of the Rule was designed essentially to restore the solitary life to a central place in monastic observance: acting upon the admission in the final chapter of the Rule that it is not meant to establish 'the full observance of righteousness', which is set out in the older ascetical literature of the desert, Romuald so organized the discipline of his monks that the common life was understood as a *preparation* for the solitary life, which was the normal and natural goal for the religious. Nor was he the only reformer to emphasize the primary importance of the eremitical life in the eleventh century: the reaction not only against 'secularization' but even against 'involvement' of the Cluniac type manifested itself in a widespread 'primitivism', an appeal to ancient models and authorities.[24] Damian is merely the most literate and articulate spokesman of the movement: it is entirely characteristic that, in one of his longer works on the eremitical life, he should appeal not only to the examples of Paul and Antony in the desert, but also to that of the prophet Elijah.[25] Romuald and Damian, and most of the other reformers, were Benedictines by profession; but the Rule is understood by them as a 'provisional' document, a beginners' guide (as, indeed, Benedict himself calls it), which requires extensive supplement, in the light both of the needs of the contemporary monastic situation and of the tradition behind Benedict himself. In fact, the presuppositions of Damian and his like are exactly those of Odo of Cluny: the Rule does not stand alone, but must be seen as the fruit and the digest of a much wider and more diversified monastic practice. The eleventh century reformers may—and do—draw very different conclusions from those of the Cluniacs; but both styles of monastic renewal look for their authority to a complex tradition crystallized in but not *circumscribed* by the Rule.[26] Again, as at Cluny, the activity of supplementing in practice takes the form of enormously detailed prescriptions concerning matters of daily life; but there is a sense in which Damian's treatise, 'On the Perfection of Monks',[27] or his works on the eremitical life, are almost independent 'rules' in themselves, as no Cluniac customary could be. This is to say, they set out a monastic ideal intentionally 'higher' than that of the Rule and, finally, independent of it. This is the essential feature of Damian's and Romuald's reformed Benedictinism—the intention ultimately to transcend the Rule in a 'more perfect' observance.

Other reformers shared this approach, in greater or lesser measure: John Gualbert, founder of the exceptionally severe Vallombrosan congregation of Benedictines, claimed to be establishing an 'exact' observance of the Rule; but, in fact, as his biography makes abundantly clear, this was a euphemism for the creation of an observance immeasurably stricter than any previous Benedictine practice, including that of Monte Cassino under Benedict. The significant expression employed by his biographer is that John 'carefully investigated the *sense* of the Rule'[28]—a 'sense' which he obviously considered to justify an exceeding of the letter of the Rule in a wide variety of ways. More eccentric by far is the attitude of that intriguing personality, Stephen of Muret, founder of the Grandmontine order. His *Liber Sententiarum* (a collection of miscellaneous instructions to his followers) begins with advice on how to reply to the question of what rule was followed in the communities of his foundation: and the answer implicitly admits that *no* conventional rule is observed, but goes on to claim that the simple and unqualified imitation of Christ's poverty and 'kenotic' humility at which they aim sets them 'outside every order and every Rule'.[29] Stephen's biographer describes him as living 'by the Rule of the Gospel, which is the chief of all rules'.[30] Evidently, Stephen's experiments caused great bewilderment at the time (though the Grandmontines soon settled into a more conventional mould): but he is perhaps no more than the most extreme expositor of the eleventh century nostalgia for evangelical purity and poverty, and the faint dissatisfaction of monastic zealots of the age with the Benedictine Rule as it stood. Stephen did, in fact, produce a 'Rule' of his own,[31] which makes no pretence of being a commentary upon or supplement to the Benedictine Rule; and virtually the same solution (though with slightly more conscious reference to the Benedictine tradition) was being adopted at almost the same time by Bruno and his 'poor men living in the desert of Chartreuse'—the future Carthusian order.

To sum up: the eleventh century reforms of the monastic institution were directed towards a radical evangelical poverty and based upon an ideal of the primitive Church and primitive monasticism. Their relation to the reforming ideals of Gregory VII is ambiguous and merits more study than it has yet received: obviously, to a man such as Damian, independence from secular control was of first importance (as it was for the Cluniacs); but Damian's ideal was intrinsically hostile to any notion that the Church should exercise secular political power 'in parallel' with the Empire or any other worldly authority. The Cluniacs and the radicals alike understood the Church in general and the monastic order in particular as the embodiment in the world of the poverty and 'service' of Christ; and though for the Cluniac this meant—let us not say 'involvement', a modish and misleading word in this context—a measure of availability, and for the radical a withdrawal into the desert, these oversimplifications cannot conceal what the two parties held in common. As we have seen, Damian was able to admire Cluny; and it is worth noting that Cluny, from its earliest days, took the eremitical life with great seriousness, and that several of its sons retired into solitude for longer or shorter periods.[32] For both groups, the Rule of St. Benedict was not an exclusive 'constitution', but a document of normative importance in establishing the basic presuppositions of monastic spirituality, whose literal prescriptions were treated with a good deal of latitude; though the modifications adopted by the different parties took very different directions. The vast and obvious divergences between the practice of Cluny and that of, say, Camaldoli or Vallombrosa should not prevent us from seeing that all belong to a single monastic 'tradition of life': if there is a debate between them, it remains implicit and, in any case, takes place within a shared mental and spiritual world.

III

Against such a background, it should be possible to see the extreme *novelty* of the Cistercian experiment. Robert of Molesme and his first followers in their writings insist again and again upon faithful adherence to the Rule, the 'integrity' of the Rule, the *rectitudo* of the Rule, observed *uno modo*.[34] Although the notorious expression *ad apicem litterae* ('to the last jot') does not appear at this early stage, it is evident that the *text* of the Rule has come to occupy a position of unprecedented and solitary eminence. This is not a peculiarity of Robert and his circle: the contemporary reforms at Tiron and Savigny in the first decade and a half of the twelfth century professed the same concern.[35] For the first time in Benedictine history, the Rule *in itself* is regarded as the norm of monastic life: Tiron, Savigny, Molesme, and Cîteaux all sought to strip away modifications and accretions in order to return to what they understood to be the exact observance of Benedict, to bypass the whole Carolingian and Cluniac tradition with its emphasis upon liturgy at the expense of manual—especially agricultural—work. Like the eleventh-century radicals, they aimed at poverty and absolute simplicity: but it was the poverty and simplicity of the Rule, not of any other primitive ideal. The tradition and the language of the 'desert' remained alive,[36] but only in strict conjunction with the prescriptions of the Rule. In practice, of course, it was recognized that precise observance of the Rule in every detail was out of the question. Several of the administrative mechanisms of the Rule—notably the council of *decani* or senior monks—were superseded, and the acceptance of lay brothers was a major departure. Vallombrosa, Grandmont, and the Chartreuse had all handed over a good deal of responsiblity (near-total in the case of Grandmont) for the daily round of business and practical administration to their lay brothers, so as to secure for the monks the *quies* necessary for contemplation: the fathers of Cîteaux followed suit, on the grounds that, without assistance from the lay brothers, they would be unable perfectly and constantly to observe the Rule[37]—a rather paradoxical justification, it might be said, but, since the lay brothers were not strictly within the monastic institution as such, it could be claimed with some plausibility that their existence was a matter which did not come within the scope of the Rule itself.

The reasons for this unprecedented preoccupation with the Rule are not immediately clear. The experience of Bernard of Tiron, for instance, suggests that in some eremitical circles there was growing dissatisfaction with the lack of an absolutely clear 'foundation-document' held in common by all; and there is evidence from other sources that there was unease in the Church at large about the proliferation of idiosyncratic hermits, wandering preachers, and new monastic congregations.[38] The wandering 'holy man', attached to no community and living by no known rule, was an obvious focus for the expression of social unrest and group hysteria, as, for instance, in the rôle played by Peter the Hermit in the first crusade; and the Church felt increasingly threatened by the volatility of its poorer children.[39] It is worth remembering that this period—the end of the eleventh and beginning of the twelfth centuries, the aftermath of the Gregorian reform—was an age of increasing *legal* consciousness in the Church: the reform and codification of canon law had been proceeding apace in the eleventh century, and was to reach a climax in the definitive work of Gratian. The Church was struggling towards a public, social, institutional self-definition: aided by the False Decretals, with their highly political account of papal power, the canonists developed a concept of the Church as a 'corporation', a quasi-state, we might say, with its own law and custom, and its own supreme court in the Papacy.[40] The idea of ecclesiastical authority operating (as I have said) 'in parallel' with secular is gaining ground at this time: and, in such a context, it is not surprising that definition and regularity should matter very greatly.

It is this, I suggest, which goes far towards providing a background for the phenomenal success of the Cistercians; though this success was actualized only by the energy and articulacy of their greatest apologist, Bernard. Of course, it would be a grave misunderstanding of Bernard to represent him as a pharisaic legalist obsessed with the letter of the Rule: his famous *Apologia*[41] explicitly rebukes the zealots of his own party who presume to condemn those whose observance is less rigorous than theirs; and its appeal is as much to a general conception of monastic integrity as to the Rule itself. Indeed, Bernard is able, in criticising the laxity of Cluny, to point to the precept and example of the great Cluniac fathers themselves.[42] Bernard does not wish all monks to be Cistercians—in theory, at least: his practice was by no means consistent with his protestations on this subject. In his treatise 'On Precept and Dispensation',[43] he distinguishes between those who have merely promised obedience 'according to the Rule'—the great mass of 'black' Benedictines, for whom a certain pluralism in observance is admissible—and the Cistercians, who are vowed to 'integral literal observance'. There is nothing *wrong* with traditional Benedictinism as such: in its own terms, it may still provide a 'school of the Lord's service'. But the Cistercian observance is of a rather different order; the treatise only deals in detail with what might be called the minimum requirements of obedience for Benedictines in general, and Bernard clearly would not have applied it as it stood to Cistercian life. The whole discussion turns on the legal question, 'What is of obligation?' and Bernard borrows the technical language of 'Stable, firm, and fixed necessity', popularized by the great canonist Yvo of Chartres, to deal with the problem. The important point is that it is taken for granted that the Rule is law: for the black Benedictines, its obligation or 'necessity' is, in certain respects, variable at the abbot's discretion (though he is himself bound in his dispensing activity by the principle of conformity with the Rule) and the demands of charity,[45] but it is, nevertheless, a matter of public and 'contractual' obligation. For the Cistercians, presumably, the degree of variability is less; but Bernard does not go into detail about this. Bernard is not arguing for any kind of literalism or fundamentalism about the Rule: but he *is* implicity defending an understanding of it in terms of law, whether strictly or loosely interpreted.

He is not the only writer to do so; even that most un-legalistic of men, Peter the Venerable of Cluny, can speak of the Rule as 'the monks' law'.[46] Bernard, in his attitude to the Rule, demonstrates his extraordinary gift for articulating with force and clarity the assumptions of a whole age and a whole society. Cistercian monasticism, as interpreted by Bernard, caught the imagination of the twelfth century because it answered to that age's need for definition, the Christian's increasing urge to understand himself in the context of a law-governed society, capable of determining the limits and the standards of behaviour, capable of drawing *boundaries*. It is no coincidence that Bernard should be an ardent apologist for the *plenitudo potestatis*, the fullness of authority, of the See of Rome, defending its rights against the rival authority of secular princes; nor that he should be so deeply involved in the preaching of the crusade, that great expression of the recovery of collective self-confidence by the Christian Church in the West. We may note also his suspicion of the eremitical life,[47] and his almost hysterical reaction to the extreme 'radical primitivism' of Arnold of Brescia (who, for all his startling heterodoxies, has many echoes of Damian and his circle). Bernard is one of the most important 'bridges' between Gregory VII and Innocent III in the development of the theocratic ideal in the Middle Ages, the ideal of the Church's political authority over the world; we are in a different spiritual world from that of either Cluny or Camaldoli, as Morghen has very lucidly pointed out.[48]

There is perhaps less difference between Peter the Venerable and Bernard than is generally supposed; but Peter can still, on occasion, be the spokesman for an older set of monastic values. Bernard, as we have seen, allows dispensation for the sake of charity, and, indeed, states that the life of charity is the purpose of the Rule;[49] Peter goes a little further, coming very close to making a distinction between Law and Gospel. No rule is above the Gospel, no monastic vow can ever be allowed to negate the Gospel;[50] the 'law' which ultimately matters is Christ's law of charity and the bearing of one another's burdens.[51] All the Law and the Prophets hang upon the commandment of love, and so, therefore, must the 'law of the rule'.[52] Now this is not merely to say that charity is an excuse for dispensations: it is to say—with Stephen of Muret—that the order of love is something other and higher than obedience to the written code. Peter may have sometimes attempted to defend the indefensible in Cluniac practice (and he was later to introduce severe reforms), but it is a mistake to imagine that his conception of charity is sentimental or merely humanistic. He states quite plainly the identity of charity with the indwelling Holy Spirit:[53] charity simply *is* the life of grace, a life beyond the Law. Not that Peter is unconcerned with the right observance of the Rule; rather, like his predecessors, he insists that it must, finally, point beyond itself. With what must surely be a conscious irony, he picks up the favourite Cistercian expression, *rectitudo regulae*, 'the righteousness (or integrity) of the Rule', and, agreeing that the Rule cannot survive if its *rectitudo* is absent, simply identifies this *rectitudo* with *caritas*.[54]

* * * * *

Charity, the law of Christ, the indwelling of the Spirit—by these the Church in general and the monastic institution in particular lives; and they are not matters which can be guaranteed by law or translated into the foundation of any political authority. I have, in these pages, sought to show that the quest for monastic renewal in the early Middle Ages is inseparably connected with the development of different conceptions of the Church's relation to the world; and so, finally, with the problem of the nature of the Church itself, and of authority in the Church. My suggestion is that the earliest essays in reform, and the radicalism of the eleventh century, are at one in maintaining a view of the Church and the monastic order as an eschatological 'sign' in the secular world, expressing the profoundly non-worldly standards of the Gospel—selfless charity, peace, poverty, humility; and that the twelfth-century developments in which Bernard took so prominent a part tended (inevitably) towards an attempt at crystallizing this in an institution with a legal polity recognizably analogous to that of a secular kingdom. This is not to pass adverse judgment upon Bernard: without the confident sense of belonging to a well-defined 'Christendom' which the twelfth century did so much to establish, the great spiritual and intellectual achievement of the High Middle Ages would have been unthinkable. Again, Bernard himself was no stranger to the idea of the eschatological 'folly' of the monastic life,[55] and, in his sermons on the Canticle and the treatise 'On Loving God', he has left us some of the finest analyses of the life of supernatural charity to come from the pen of any Christian writer. Nevertheless, it is difficult not to feel that something has been lost, that a decay in the proper understanding of the Mystical Body has set in: Innocent III is a good deal further from the New Testament than is, say, Odo, or Damian. Historically intelligible, if not unavoidable, it is nonetheless theologically deplorable. Bernard is not only the last of the fathers; he is one of the first great ideologists of the mediaeval Western church, and we should not forget this side of him. And, in the hard and even bitter task of purifying and renewing our understanding of Christian and religious life in the desperate climate of this century, it may help to go back decisively beyond this mediaeval model of Church and society, to the bleaker world which produced Cluny and Camaldoli. What, one wonders, might Peter Damian and Dietrich Bonhoeffer have had to say to one another?

* * * * *

NOTES

1. An indebtedness amply demonstrated in many papers presented at the Orthodox-Cistercian Colloquium held at Oxford in 1973, published in *Two Yet One*, 2 vols., B. Pennington (ed.), Cistercian Publications 1976.

2. It seems now to be fairly generally accepted that there was a real continuity between the Carolingian reforms and the Cluniac; see, e.g., D. Knowles, *The Monastic Order in England* (2nd ed. Cambridge, 1949), pp. 29-30; N. Hunt (ed.),

Cluniac Monasticism in the Central Middle Ages, London 1971, pp. 4-5.

3. Op. cit., pp. 18-20.

4. On this, see Dom A. de Vogüé's excellent discussion, 'Sub Regula uel Abbate' in *Rule and Life: an Interdisciplinary Symposium*, ed. M.B. Pennington, OCSO (Cistercian Publications 1972), pp. 21-63.

5. 'A careful gathering of tradition, ancient and modern, written and lived' (Knowles, op. cit., p. 26). For a summary of these interpretations, see Benedict of Aniane's *Codex Regularum* and *Concordia Regularum*, Migne, PL 103.

6. '*Le monachisme à l'apparition de Bernard*' (in *Bernard de Clairvaux, Commission d'histoire de l'Ordre de Citeaux*, Paris, 1953, pp. 45-63), pp. 47-48, n. 16.

7. Dom Jean Leclercq has argued that, at this time, 'custom' was still evaluated according to its 'conformity to the fundamental observances established by RB [the Rule]' ('Profession According to the Rule of St. Benedict', in *Rule and Life*, pp. 117-149; see esp. pp. 119-124); but I am not quite sure what this means. The material which he discusses suggests rather that the monks of this period would not have been *able* to separate Rule and custom to the extent of using one as a criterion for judging the other.

8. PL 133, col. 723-724.

9. Op. cit., pp. 29-30, and c.f. p. 20.

10. PL 133, col. 59.

11. L.M. Smith, *The Early History of the Monastery of Cluny* (Oxford 1920), pp. 182-184, gives a useful summary of the Cluniac tradition concerning the origin of this practice.

12. Knowles, op. cit., p. 45. See also his *Christian Monasticism* (London, Weidenfeld & Nicolson, 1969), pp. 217-18, for the timetable of such a house in the eleventh century, which gives a vivid impression of the proportion of the day allotted to public 'intercession' by means of psalmody over and above that of the Office.

13. See the admirable essays in Hunt, op. cit., by R. Morghen and Dom Kassius Hallinger on Cluniac spirituality.

14. PL 133, 64-66, for Odo's exertions in this sphere.

15. Smith, op. cit., pp. 170-182, surveys the various attempts which led up to the

formulation of the terms of the Truce itself (a suspension of violent and belligerent activity each week from sunset on Wednesday to dawn on Monday).

16. For Odo's personal charity to the poor, a charity of almost Franciscan scale, see PL 133, 62-63.

17. The best general survey is still Ernst Sackur's *Die Cluniacenser* (2 vols., Halle, 1892 and 1894) though a great many of his judgments are no longer acceptable; on monastic reform movements, see especially vol. I, chs. 2, 3, 6, and 8, vol. II, chs. 2, 5, 7, 10, and 13. On the great rôle played by Abbot Odilo in the eleventh century, see vol. II, pp. 298-302; Sackur compares his importance to that of Bernard in the twelfth century (p. 299).

18. Hunt, op. cit., pp. 18ff.

19. See, e.g., P. Evdokimov, *The Struggle with God*, pp. 93ff.

20. For St. Luke's Day; Serm. LIII, PL 144, 806C.

21. Ep. Lib. VI, no. xxvii, PL 144, 416 BC.

22. Opusculum XXVIII, PL 145, 511D-512D.

23. A useful study of Damian's general thinking on this subject may be found in *Hildebrandine Essays*, by J.P. Whitney (Cambridge, 1932), pp. 95-142 ('Peter Damiani and Humbert'); and in *Church, State and Christian Society at the Time of the Investiture Contest*, by G. Tellenbach (Oxford, 1948), pp. 67-8, there is a summary of Damian's views on clerical non-violence.

24. On the hermit movement of the period, see Sackur, op cit., I, pp. 323-334, and Louis Lekai, S.O. Cist., 'Motives and Ideals of the Eleventh Century Monastic Renewal', in *The Cistercian Spirit: a Symposium in Memory of Thomas Merton*, ed. M.B. Pennington, OCSO (Cistercian Publication, 1970), pp. 27-47—a very valuable essay.

25. Opusculum XV, cap. II, PL 145, 337C-338A.

26. Lekai, op. cit., pp. 40-42, rightly warns against attributing anything like a modern historical consciousness to the eleventh century primitivists; but the seriousness of their appeal to antiquity (however imperfectly that antiquity was understood) is not to be disregarded.

27. Opusculum XIII, PL 145.

28, PL 146, 775; I cannot quite agree with Lekai's understanding of this (op.

cit., p. 43).

29. PL 204, 1085C-1087D.

30. Ibid., 1024.

31. Ibid., 1135C-1162B.

32. See J. Leclercq, 'Pierre le Vénérable et l'érémitisme clunsisien, in *Petrus Venerabilis*, ed. by G. Constable and J. Kritzeck (Rome, *Studia Anselmiana*, 1956), pp. 99-120, esp. pp. 106-112.

33. Dom Leclercq, in 'The Intentions of the Founders of the Cistercian Order' (*The Cistercian Spirit*, pp. 88-133), summarizes the most important of these documents, with extensive quotation (pp. 90-101).

34. Ibid., p. 99.

35. Interestingly, Bernard of Tiron and Vitalis of Savigny both emerged from a group of eremitical 'radicals'. Also, Bernard in particular was openly hostile to Cluny: a sign of the changing times (see Knowles, *The Monastic Order*, pp. 200-202).

36. See Leclercq, 'Intentions', p. 92.

37. *Exordium Parvum Cisterciense*, ch. 15 (ed. J.B. Van Damme, *Documenta pro Cisterciensis Ordinis Historiae ac Juris Studio*, Westmalle, 1959, p. 13).

38. See 'Cîteaux et le Règle dans le context du XIe siècle', by Lin Donnat, OSB (*Collectanea Cisterciensia*, 1973, vol. 35, no. 3, pp. 161-172), pp. 165-168.

39. E. Werner's Marxist interpretation of the monastic reform movement (*Pauperes Christi*, Berlin, 1956) has much to contribute to our understanding of this; though his general thesis is a gross oversimplification.

40. See Whitney, *Hildebrandine Essays*, pp. 13ff., W. Ullmann, *A Short History of the Papacy in the Middle Ages* (London, Methuen, 1972), chs. 7 and 8, etc.

41. Translated in vol. I of *The Works of Bernard of Clairvaux* (Cistercian Publications, 1970), pp. 33-69.

42. *Apologia*, 23 (ed. cit., p. 59).

43. *Works*, vol. I, pp. 105-150.

44. Chs. 48-49 (p. 141).

45. Chs. 4-5 (pp. 108-109).

46. *The Letters of Peter the Venerable*, ed. by G. Constable (Harvard, 1967); Letter 58, vol. I, p. 184.

47. See, e.g., Letter 118, in *The Letters of Saint Bernard of Clairvaux*, ed. and tr. by B. Scott James (London, Burns & Oates, 1953), pp. 179-180.

48. Hunt, op. cit., p. 28.

49. *On Precept and Dispensation*, chs. 5 and 9 (pp. 108-109, 111).

50. Letter 28 (ed. cit., I, p. 59).

51. Letter 111 (ibid., p. 278).

52. Ibid. (p. 285).

53. Letter 28 (ibid., pp. 98-99).

54. Ibid. (p. 90).

55. See esp. Letter 90 (ed. cit., p. 135).

ST. BERNARD AND ST. GILBERT[1]

Brian Golding

THE GENERAL CHAPTER that met at Cîteaux in September 1147 was no ordinary chapter. Those present included, besides Bernard and the other Cistercian abbots, Pope Eugenius III, 'not presiding by apostolic authority, but staying amongst them, as one of them, in brotherly love', two heads of independent orders, the abbot of Savigny and Stephen, abbot of Obazine, who had come in order to cede their houses to the Cistercian order, and Raymond, the future Master of the Templars.[2] The assembly was, then, a roll-call of those whom Bernard had, in one way or another, directly influenced. Another 'observer' at Cîteaux may have been less obvious and his presence there at first sight hard to explain. Gilbert of Sempringham was a little known priest of distant Lincolnshire and the leader, much against his will, of a community of nuns and lay brothers and sisters. This small community had as yet no rule. Gilbert had come to ask the Cistercians to take over his group and to allow him once more to retire into obscurity. As far as is known he had never received any letter from Bernard nor written a letter to the abbot of Clairvaux, and in all probability this was the first time they had met; yet by the close of the chapter a close friendship between the two had sprung up. By the time of Innocent III's confirmation of the Gilbertines' privileges Bernard was being described as *co-founder* of the order.[3] However, when the past history of Gilbert is considered, together with the lay and spiritual ties that bound the society of Lincolnshire and Yorkshire together, his appearance at Cîteaux in 1147 is perhaps not so remarkable.

On his return from studies in France, his father, Jocelin, had given Gilbert his two proprietary churches of Sempringham and West Torrington on the Lincolnshire estates that Jocelin held of earl Gilbert de Gant.[4] Though he had not yet been ordained priest, Gilbert proceeded to reform the parish of Sempringham and also to hold a school for village children where they could gain a rudimentary education. He also followed as far as he was able the rules of a religious life and kept monastic hours. He remained at Semprinham until, on coming to the notice of Robert Bloet, bishop of Lincoln, he moved to Lincoln to serve as a clerk in the bishop's household. When Robert died in 1123 Gilbert stayed on in the *familia* of his successor, Bishop Alexander the Magnificent, where he acquired a reputation for austerity and charity, and where, much against his will, he was ordained priest. It was as a member of the *familia* of the bishops of Lincoln that Gilbert moved onto a wider stage, and though he turned down the offer of high office in the diocese, his association with Alexander was enough to ensure a growing influence and fame. Alexander's spirituality, like that of so many of his contemporary prelates, was ambiguous. On the one hand, he was a great temporal power, the counsellor of kings, immensely wealthy and the patron of writers such as Henry of Huntingdom; on the other, he appears as a founder of monasteries, the patron of hermits, the supporter of reformers and the friend of Eugenius III.[5] By 1140 he had founded at least three monasteries. Both William of Newburgh and Gerald of Wales suggest that the motive for these foundations was merely expiatory, Gerald going so far as to suggest that they were financed from the resources of Lincoln cathedral rather than from his own private funds.[6] Yet this interpretation is perhaps over-simplistic; these two aspects of the character of Alexander, as of Thurstan of York, for example, whom he closely resembles, are symptomatic of inner tensions between the quasi-secular and the religious roles which the bishop was expected to fulfil. To Bernard, however, the character of the bishop was clear and unambiguous. It is unknown when Alexander first came to the notice of Bernard, but around 1129 he was the recipient of a letter from the abbot describing how one, Philip, who appears to have been a member of the episcopal household, and, hence, a companion of Gilbert, while on pilgrimage to Jerusalem had diverted his journey to Clairvaux where he had remained, finding there his spiritual Jerusalem.[7] The winds of reform were blowing even in the household of Alexander. This event, which occured before any Cistercian houses were founded in the diocese of Lincoln, and probably only a year after the foundation of Waverley, the first English Cistercian house, was probably Gilbert's introduction to the Cistercians in general and to the abbot of Clairvaux in particular.

Shortly afterwards Gilbert left Lincoln for his native Sempringham. While at Lincoln he had already been following a life more like that of a regular canon or monk than that of a secular priest, and when he arrived at Sempringham he founded his first community with the aid and advice of his bishop. This community for seven maidens adjoined the north wall of the parish church of St. Andrew. It had no rule but that of charity, chastity, humility and obedience. Gilbert arranged for girls of the parish to attend to the daily needs of his nuns. He was, however, warned by friends that this arrangement might lead to the corruption of the community and that problems of discipline might arise. While considering these problems he met William, the first abbot of Rievaulx, who was passing through Lincolnshire, perhaps either on his way to or from a general chapter at Cîteaux, or possibly coming from France to settle at the new foundation in 1132. Now William had been Bernard's secretary at Clairvaux and it was William who suggested a solution. The serving women were incorporated into the community as lay-sisters, a move that they themselves welcomed eagerly. At the same time Gilbert noted that William had with him some Cistercian lay-brothers, and this innovation too was adopted by the house at Sempringham, Gilbert's lay-brothers following the Cistercian rule. Thus already in the very early years of the order the Cistercian influence was strong, even before the Gilbertines had their own rule.[8] Though Gilbert had not yet met Bernard, his influence was felt.

For some years there were no further Gilbertine foundations, but in 1137 Bishop Alexander offered the marshy island of Haverholme, near Sleaford, to the abbot of Fountains to create a daughter house there. This was accepted and building commenced. After two years the buildings were ready and a colony was sent out from Fountains. On their arrival, however, the site displeased them. No reasons were given for the Cistercian rejection of Haverholme; the most likely explanation seems to be that the marshy site was ill-suited to intensive sheep farming.[9] At any rate Alexander offered the monks instead his land at Louth Park and this became the second Cistercian house in Lincolnshire. Alexander gave Haverholme instead to the nuns which were 'under the care and teaching of Gilbert the priest', who followed 'the strict life, the holy life, that is, the life of the monks of Cîteaux as far as the strength of their sex allowed'.[10] At this time, then, it seems clear that Gilbert's communities were following, with some modifications, the Cistercian rule and that, indeed, they were considered to be Cistercians.

Gilbert himself accepted no new foundations until after 1147, but all around him the Lincolnshire Cistercian monasteries were springing up. Kirkstead and Louth Park were founded in 1139, Revesby followed in 1143 and Bytham (which moved to Vaudey in 1149) in 1147. All of these were colonised from Fountains with the exception of Revesby, which came from Rievaulx with Aelred.[11] In no county was the growth of religious communities during the reign of Stephen so marked as it was in Lincolnshire, and nowhere, not even in Yorkshire, did the 'new' orders make greater advances than here.[12] It is in this atmosphere of burgeoning enthusiasm that Gilbert worked during the 1140's. A priest and ascetic with definite leanings towards the eremitical life, he found himself the head of two communities which even lacked a certain rule; in practice Cistercian, but in no way formally affiliated to them. There is no doubt, however, that Gilbert's foundations were popular. His biographer describes how the houses 'grew under the patronage of many rich and noble earls and barons who showered money and possessions on him and built many houses throughout many districts', with the king himself as the foremost patron. Here Gilbert's biographer exaggerates, for it seems unlikely that any more Gilbertine houses were founded until 1148, but there is no doubt that Gilbert's popularity placed him in a quandary. The author of the Life goes on to state that Gilbert refused many gifts since he loved humility and poverty: but there was little he could do, for his foundations fulfilled a real need. Alone of the 'new' orders they gave a place to women, only the most aristocratic of whom were served by the Benedictine nunneries which were still the almost exclusive preserve of daughters of the wealthy. Gilbert found a place for village girls as well as for the daughters of the local gentry. His appeal was always to be predominantly local, indeed parochial, and this 'grass-roots' support was to be one of the major factors of Gilbert's success.[13]

One final aspect of the background to 1147 remains to be considered. The patrons of the Lincolnshire Cistercian houses were the local gentry, the class on whom Gilbert would rely heavily for support. Moreover, close ties bound the landowners of Lincolnshire and Yorkshire together. Just as Gilbert knew both William and Aelred of Rievaulx in Yorkshire, so too his lay patrons often had interests, both personal and landed, on both sides of the Humber. One example of the ties between the counties—and one that reveals a link Bernard had with the laity as well as with the clergy of Yorkshire—concerns the oligarchy of Beverley. To Thomas, the provost of that town, Bernard wrote two of his most famous letters urging him not to turn from his earlier declared intention of becoming a Cistercian monk. The later history of Thomas is unknown, but he may well have been the father of Mabel, who married Hamelin, the dean, a leading cleric and one of the founders of the Gilbertine house of Alvingham in North Lincolnshire soon after 1148.[14]

Gilbert increasingly felt that he ought to place his communities under the care of others. He quoted the words of Moses that he had, by becoming a ruler of men and by being forced to engage in secular conversation, become a lesser and less holy man. He was ill and also comparatively old (though he was in the event to live on until 1189). Sometime in 1147 Gilbert heard of the forthcoming chapter to be held at Cîteaux in September. He accordingly journeyed there in order to place his congregation in the hands of the order with which he already had such strong ties. His *Life* states that he came to the Cistercians rather than to any other order since he judged them to be stricter and more religious than other orders, and also because he had frequently been a guest of theirs. The Latin here is ambiguous; it could imply that Gilbert had actually visited Cîteaux earlier (presumably while he had been studying in France), but more probably it means merely that he had stayed with Cistercian communities in England.[15] In September Gilbert offered his people to Eugenius and the assembled abbots. Their answer, however, was disappointing. They judged that it was not right that Cistercian abbots should take over the governance of another order, especially since that order included women. Now the position of Cistercian nunneries was to remain uncertain for many years, but it seems that the chapter's answer did not represent the whole truth. There were, after all, at least two Cistercian nunneries in Lincolnshire by this date and, further, they must have had an organization that in all essentials was the same as that of Sempringham and Haverholme.[16] Moreover, to describe Gilbert's communities as another order when it had as yet no distinct rule and relied so heavily upon the Cistercians was not entirely accurate. The real reason for the refusal to undertake the government of Gilbert's foundations was probably the fact that it was at this chapter that the Cistercians received the houses of both the Savignac and the Obazine order, an accession which considerably increased the order's responsibilities.[17] In this situation, the taking on of further responsibilities for communities that were clearly flourishing under capable, though unwilling, leadership, may well have seemed unnecessary and ill-advised. This failure to undertake the rule of Gilbert's houses may well be the reason for the omission of all mention of Gilbert's presence at the chapter in Cistercian sources. The only account of Gilbert's visit is contained in his *Life*, though William of Newburgh also speaks of the support given him by Bernard in drawing up the rule of his order.[18]

Instead of achieving his purpose of relinquishing his communities and returning to the life of a solitary and contemplative, Gilbert found himself made master over his congregation by the command of Eugenius, in spite of his complaints that he was unworthy, unlearned, and aged. Eugenius's high opinion of Gilbert is revealed by a comment he is alleged to have made at the chapter, that, had he known Gilbert earlier he would have promoted him to the vacant archbishopric of York, a position for which Gilbert would have felt himself even more unfitted.

Little is known of Gilbert's movements following the chapter, but at some time between September 1147 and November 1148 he and Bernard together drew up the Gilbertine rule. Also present, and an adviser, was Archbishop Malachy of Armagh. Malachy is not known to have arrived at Clairvaux until October 1148, a month before he died, so it must be supposed that Gilbert remained at Clairvaux for over a year, though Bernard himself is known not to have been at his abbey often during 1147 and 1148.[19] During this time Gilbert clearly came to know the Cistercian rule well, and these months of which so little is known proved crucial for the future history of his order. For it was here that the decision was made to add a fourth rank to his congregation, that of the canons who would serve the nuns and would themselves follow the Augustinian rule. It is difficult to evaluate the precise role played by Bernard and the Cistercians in drawing up the Gilbertine Constitutions, for they were so eclectic, borrowing widely for the rules governing each of the four divisions of the Gilbertine personnel. Certainly, in the Prologue to the Rule Gilbert acknowledged the key role played by the Cistercians, but against this must be set the fact that the rules of the canons owed nothing to the Cistercians and that for the nuns Bernard and Gilbert had little on which to base their rule, since regulations for Cistercian nuns had not as yet been drawn up. For his nuns Gilbert used the Benedictine rule but adapted it to a greater severity on two issues that probably owed much to early Cistercian practice. His nuns were to be rigorously enclosed, and a significant portion of the rule is taken up with elaborate rules for ensuring complete seclusion from the world. Moreover, chants and all manner of musical instruments were absolutely forbidden. Here, as elsewhere, however, it is impossible to state conclusively whether the initiative for severity came from Gilbert or Bernard. The reliance upon the Cistercians is more clearly seen in the rule for the *conversi* where the two rules are almost verbally identical in many places. A word of caution is necessary here, however, for surviving copies of the Gilbertine rule all post-date the lay-brothers' revolt of the late 1160's, after which Gilbert is known to have modified the severity of those sections of his rule that dealt with the *conversi*.[20]

The influence of the Cistercians is more clearly seen in the general organization and administration of the order. The same limitations and regulations were placed upon the establishment of new foundations; the institution of the general chapter to be held annually at Sempringham is clearly copied from the Cistercian model, and the section on the unity of the order shows in a mistake of terminology the direct verbal borrowing from the older order, for it refers to the unity of the abbeys (*recte* priories). The centralized organization of the Gilbertines went altogether further than did the Cistercian practice, for though Dom David Knowles was right when he wrote, 'Constitutionally regarded Gilbert's family was less of an order than the Cistercians; it was a federation of Benedictine nunneries served by groups of canons and lay brothers guided by a master', the important innovation of the Gilbertines was the introduction of a single supreme head, the Master of the Order, who, after Gilbert's death, while living at Sempringham was not always also prior of Sempringham.[21] In a rule as eclectic as that of Sempringham, perhaps the most important contribution of the Cistercians was, in a more general sense, the way of life followed by the new order which is shown both in the overall tone of the Constitutions and in specific rulings which reflect contemporary Cistercian practice. In the matter of vestments and of food there is the same austerity and simplicity. The Gilbertine service books were, in accordance with Cistercian custom, to be identical with each other in each house, and in matters of church architecture and furnishings the same austerity was to be practised. Superfluous pictures and sculptures were forbidden because they diverted and distracted the mind from contemplation.

When Gilbert left Clairvaux, both Bernard and Malachy gave him the staves of their croziers as tokens of love, and Bernard in addition gave him a reliquary. Gilbert returned, frustrated in his purpose, to England, and from this date the order's expansion really began. By 1160 seven houses for canons and nuns had been founded besides two for canons alone.[22] The close connection between the order and the Cistercians continued. Gilbert became an intimate friend of Aelred of Rievaulx, and the latter played a crucial role later in the sad story of the nun of the Gilbertine house in Watton in Yorkshire, when he was called in by Gilbert as an adviser.[23] Many of the Gilbertine houses were founded by men who were also founders and enthusiastic benefactors of Cistercian houses, and there was little to choose between the two in terms either of their spirituality or their economic organization. Such closeness could lead to great friendship, such as that which existed between Gilbert and Aelred; it could also produce great rivalry where Gilbertines and Cistercians competed for the same type of grants from the same benefactors. In order to obviate such competition an agreement was signed in 1164 between the general chapter of Cîteaux and Sempringham, Aelred leading the Cistercian and Gilbert the Gilbertine delegation. It stipulated that in future no house might build a grange or sheep-fold within two leagues of an already existing grange or sheep-fold of the other order. Careful rules were drawn up to ensure that any disputes should be settled within the confines of the two orders rather than making them subject to external arbitration. Similar agreements were also drawn up between individual houses that lay close to each other. Barely a mile separates Cistercian Louth Park from Gilbertine Alvingham, and in 1174 they made an agreement concerning the acquisition of lands in which the arbiters were to be the Cistercian abbots of Fountains, Kirkstead, and Revesby and the Gilbertine priors of Haverholme and Sixle.[24] Even at the end of the twelfth century, and beyond, there seems to have been little to distinguish Cistercian nunneries from their Gilbertine counterparts. Writing around 1200, Gervase of Canterbury described the Lincolnshire Cistercian houses of Stixwould and Nun Cotham as containing *canonici albi et moniales*, the same term as he uses to describe neighbouring Gilbertine houses. He also used the term *canonici albi* to describe Premonstratensian canons. To confound confusion, the Gilbertine house of Shouldham in Norfolk was said to contain *moniales albae*, the term he uses elsewhere to describe Cistercian nuns.[25] As late as 1270 the abbot of Cîteaux was complaining to the dean of Lincoln that though six abbesses of Lincolnshire houses wore the Cistercian habit, they did not belong to his order. There have been later suggestions that these houses were, in fact, Gilbertine, but there is no certain knowledge either way.[26] What these incidents do reveal is that for many, including the orders themselves, a very real doubt existed as to which order a nunnery of the 'new' orders owed allegiance. It was, perhaps, an inevitable consequence of the Cistercian involvement in the creation of Gilbert's rule.

To assess the precise role played by Bernard in the creation of the Gilbertine rule is doubly difficult. Firstly, both he and Gilbert were representatives of the same spirituality. While it is true that Gilbert remained more closely linked with the eremitical life and his whole career shows that he considered himself first and foremost a solitary and contemplative, Bernard, too, while realizing the dangers and temptations of the solitary state, yet gave considerable support and advice both to individual hermits and groups of hermits.[27] Within a monastic framework, while Bernard's organizational powers were greater than those of Gilbert whose first impulse always seems to have been to avoid institutions and organizations on the grounds that they deflected him from his solitary vocation, their attitude to the religious life was essentially the same. Secondly, the Gilbertine rule was such an amalgam of other rules that it is difficult to separate out the direct Cistercian influence. It is perhaps futile to categorize the different strands that went to make up the Gilbertine Constitutions; they derive from the Benedictine rule, Premonstratensian, Grandmontine, Augustinian and the order of Fontevrault's practices as well as from the Cistercian. All are adapted to fit the peculiar condition of communities that are essentially of strictly enclosed nuns served by chaplains and laybrothers. A similar pattern is apparent from the Use of the order which again shows considerable Cistercian influence but also important borrowings from the uses of other orders.[28] Yet it is certain that without the impulse of Bernard (and also of Eugenius III) the Gilbertine communities would not have survived. Unorganized in 1147, by the end of Gilbert's life his biographer states that there were 2,200 members of the order. This may be an exaggeration, but it cannot be denied that in the late twelfth century the Gilbertines were the fastest growing order in England. Gilbert had never wanted to found an order at all. Had he succeeded in persuading Bernard and the Cistercians at Cîteaux to take over responsibility for his family, and had he not then been actively encouraged and aided by Bernard in the construction of a framework for his communities, his unique expression of English monasticism would never have been born. The influence of St. Bernard upon the Gilbertine order is perhaps less obvious than it was upon other orders but it was no less real.

* * * * *

NOTES

1. The most accessible account of the life of St. Gilbert is in R. Graham, *S. Gilbert of Sempringham and the Gilbertines* (London 1903). The Latin 'Life of Saint Gilbert' on which the narrative in Miss Graham's study is based is transcribed in W. Dugdale, *Monasticon Anglicanum* (London 1830), vol.6, part ii, interpolated between pages 945 and 946. The Institutions of the Gilbertine order are also given here immediately following the Life. The only essay on the relations between St. Bernard and the Gilbertines is by F. Giraudot and J. de la Croix Bouton

in *Bernard de Clairvaux* (1953), 327-38.

2. D.J. Canivez, *Statuta Capitulorum Generalium Ordinis Cisterciensis ab anno 1116 ad annum 1789* (1933), i, 37-8.

3. Dugdale, op. cit., vol. 6, part ii, 961.

4. For the de Gants' extensive holdings in Lincolnshire in 1086 see *The Lincoln Domesday and the Lindsay Survey*, ed. C.W. Foster and T. Longley (Lincoln Record Society, 19, 1924), 105-15.

5. *Dictionary of National Biography*, vol. 1, 267-71.

6. Giraldus Cambrensis, *Vita S. Remigii* (Rolls Series, 1877), 33; and William of Newburgh, *Historia Rerum Anglicanum* (Rolls Series, 1884), 37.

7. P. L., clxxxii, vol. i, 169-70.

8. Graham, op. cit., 11-12.

9. Dugdale, op. cit., vol. 5, 414.

10. Ibid., vol. 6, part ii, 948-9.

11. D. Knowles and R. Neville Hadcock, *Medieval Religious Houses, England and Wales* (London, 1971), 115-28, *passim*.

12. For general accounts of Lincolnshire ecclesiastical history in this period, see V.C.H. *Lincolnshire*, ed. W. Page (London, 1906), vol. 2, *passim*, and D.M. Owen, *Church and Society in Medieval Lincolnshire* (Lincoln, 1971).

13. This local appeal is reflected in a different context in the miracle stories of St. Gilbert. See R. Foreville, *Le Livre de Saint Gilbert de Sempringham* (1943).

14. P. L., op. cit., 242-9, 619-22. Dugdale, op. cit., vol. 6, part ii, 957-8.

15. *Hos enim caeteris habuit, ex frequenti hospicii susceptione, familiores.*

16. For a brief discussion of this topic see Knowles and Hadcock, op. cit., 271.

17. Canivez, op. cit., vol. i, 37-8.

18. William of Newburgh, op. cit., 54-5.

19. E. Vacandard, *La Vie de Saint Bernard* (Paris, 1920), *passim*.

20. Graham, op. cit., 19-23.

21. D. Knowles, *From Pachomius to Ignatius, a Study in the Constitutional History of the Religious Orders* (Oxford, 1966), 35-6; and D. Knowles, C.N.L.Brooke and V.C.M. London, *The Heads of Religious Houses, England and Wales, 940-1210* (Cambridge, 1972), 204-5.

22. Knowles and Hadcock, op. cit., 184-99.

23. See Aelred's tract, *De Sanctimoniali de Watton*, P.L., cxcv, 789-95; and *Life of St. Aelred of Rievaulx*, ed. F.M. Powicke (London, 1950), lxxxi-ii.

24. Graham, op. cit., 128-30.

25. Gervase of Canterbury, *Opera* (Rolls Series, 1880), 429, 428.

26. *Calendar of Charter Rolls, 1268-72*, 301. Quoted and commented upon in Knowles and Hadcock, op. cit., 271.

27. See J.Gillon in *Bernard de Clairvaux* (1953), 251-62.

28. *The Gilbertine Use* has been published for the Henry Bradshaw Society in an edition by R.M. Woolley (Henry Bradshaw Society, l and li, 1921 and 1922). See especially the introduction in vol. 1, xxv-ix.

THE KNIGHTS OF GOD
CITEAUX AND THE QUEST OF THE HOLY GRAIL

Sister Isabel Mary, SLG

Not everything has a name. Some things lead us into a realm beyond words. Art thaws even the frozen darkened soul, opening it to lofty spiritual experience. Through Art we are sometimes sent—indistinctly, briefly—revelations not to be achieved by rational thought.

A. Solzhenitzyn: 'One Word of Truth'

IN THE QUIET SICK-ROOM of an abbey, a monk is explaining with kindly patience the cause of his misadventure to a wounded knight. He has, it appears, taken the wrong turning. His real road had lain to the right, 'in the way of Jesus Christ, the way of compassion, in which the knights of Our Lord travel by night and day in the darkness of the body and the soul's light.' (p. 70)[1]

The Holy Grail lies at the heart of the Matter of Britain like the captain jewel in a setting of rich and random intricacy, and the *Quest* finds a way to it that is austere and narrow but arterially direct. No artist in any language, inspired by the Grail, has followed it farther than the French Clerk who looked through a lancet window on the mystery of the soul's ascent to God. It was the creature of his inventive genius and his didactic daring and no other's, that achieved the glorious Vessel. Galahad has had no successors, nor any rivals, for he disarms competition as he declines company. What has been said of the Grail itself may be said of him: '*Sui generis* he stands alone', not in virtue of isolation, but as an image of the normal Christian man in tranquil possession of his end.

Such was the outcome of a single-minded obedience to vision, which chose from an exuberant tangle of material only what could be made to bear the consecrating light that pierces sea and land from the far country to which Galahad so passionately tends. The *Quest* is by every token an Arthurian adventure, but at the same time an ascetic manual, a brilliant fiction and the apotheosis of a saint, a Romantic allegory and 'a Cistercian document'.

I

It was written in the first quarter of the thirteenth century, at a period when two ideals, apparently irreconcileable, had gained a firm hold on the imagination of Western Europe.

In consequence, on the one hand, of the reformed monastic life of Cîteaux and its contagious spiritual vitality, the Church had been washed with one of those periodic 'tides of recognition' that the life of a Christian is nothing less than a perpetually renewed response to the Divine Love that created him, redeemed him and invites him unwearyingly to claim to the utmost the mercy offered him—a share in the very nature and life of God Himself. This is the inexhaustible theme of St. Bernard and the whole Cistercian school.

At the same time, another ideal, indeed a religion, of Courtly Love seemed to offer a *modus vivendi* to men and women consumed with desire for each other but trapped like song-birds in the cages of feudal society. To speak all too summarily of a vast and many-sided theme, the love in question, relieved of its forms and rituals, is the desire to possess and enjoy another being who remains forever out of the lover's reach. It is that *cupiditas* which maintains its élan by submitting to a tension in which denial is stretched to the limit of endurance, before being released in a fleeting satisfaction, experienced by the lover as rapture indeed but also as mercy and largesse.

Unashamedly at variance not only with the dismal sexual ethics of the medieval Church, but more deeply with the Christian revelation of Love, *cupiditas* confines its vassals to an orbit in which the only conflict is of one passion with another, the only issue the sorrow of the world that worketh death. Taken, however, *au grand sérieux* and penetrated by the reverence and restraint borrowed with other virtues from Christian practice, this cult of the Lady could both absorb and refine energies which might otherwise have run to waste along channels of barbarous appetite. It made Lancelots of lovesick pages, and invested simple young women with the attributes of queens. Its appeal remained irresistible and its vigour unspent almost until the middle of the present century. In Dante's vision it is St. Bernard who will show him that reconciliation among the stars 'when Love ceased to be a passion and became the energy of contemplation', but that is another and a later story. In the world of thought where St. Bernard's mind towered, though there were parleys there never could be any truce. As R.W. Southern has written: 'The religious and romantic quests were born in the same world—Troyes is only about thirty miles from Clairvaux—and drew in part on the same sources of inspiration, but they were in the twelfth century kept rigidly apart. They were, indeed, the great alternatives opened out to the imagination in the mid-twelfth century.'[2]

One sphere there was, however, in which both could find a voice. This common ground was itself a third ideal, the order of Chivalry which furnished religion and romance alike with a wealth of serviceable ideas. Since the knight had first made his appearance about the middle of the eleventh century, as a mounted fighting man, pledged, by initiation into a brotherhood, to a code of behaviour which anticipated that of the tamer 'gentleman', he had gradually gathered to himself a grave prestige, an aura of religious solemnity, which made the title indispensable for any man of birth, whatever his feudal status in terms of power and property. The order could be received only at the hands of another knight and after keeping vigil in church, and once knighted, a man must make his own way in the world, by taking the adventures and discharging the tasks which his degree laid upon him. In the *Quest*, for example, Galahad is knighted by Lancelot on the Eve of Pentecost, and a few days later he performs the same office for his squire Melias, himself a king's son.

'Good friend', says Galahad, 'since you are now a knight and spring even from royal stock, take care so to acquit yourself in the service of chivalry that your lineage forfeit none of its lustre. For when a king's son receives the order of knighthood, he must outshine all other knights in virtue, even as the sun's light makes the stars seem pale.' (p. 65)

Few knights perhaps possessed or were prepared to acquire the knightly character at this level, but by the end of the twelfth century no literate man could be ignorant of what it was meant to be, for its perfect manifestation was to be found at the Round Table, where King Arthur presided over a company of the loveliest knights in Christendom, familiar by name and exploit to all who could read, or cared to listen. There is the tale of a Cistercian abbot[3] who roused his somnolent Chapter to lively interest with the magic name of Arthur, to show that its potency was not confined to secular circles. Long before the close of the twelfth century Chrétien de Troyes had 'stamped upon men's minds indelibly the conception of Camelot as the home par excellence of true and noble love',[4] and there a restless imagination, hemmed in by the often gross and grimy realities of a career at court or in the field, might be appeased by the spectacle of Christian knighthood forever probing a world of boundless opportunity.

What the Round Table was for the layman, the picture of the armed Christian in the Letter to the Ephesians (6:10-18) was for the Cistercian. For all its magnetic novelty, the Reform had no object beyond that of a literal fidelity to St. Benedict's Rule—bearing always in mind the unspeakable promises that waited on the far side of obedience—and most of its early struggles were devoted to securing conditions in which such fidelity might be something more than a wistful hope. The military metaphor was already there in the Prologue to the Rule, and it became the characteristic of the ascetic idiom of the young Reform with its insistence on the vigilance and endurance proper to the soldier and the monk:

> To you therefore my words are now addressed, whoever you are, that renouncing your own will, you do take up the strong and bright weapons of obedience, in order to fight for the Lord Christ, our true King.

A metaphor always in use and expanded into an allegory which conceived the world as a battlefield where every man engaged in a personal struggle for holiness was to become substantial reality with the foundation of the military orders.

II

The twelfth century Crusades suddenly sprang upon the chivalry of Europe an adventure almost Arthurian in its scope and its appeal to the imagination. All that was denied an unremarkable or hard-up knight at home was waiting for him in the remote strangeness of the East, where he was summoned as a deliverer by the Vicar of Christ himself. Not only the brave and pious kindled to the appeal of Urban II, or followed, two centuries later, the oriflamme of St. Louis, but from the start, landless younger sons and well-born bullies could be lured from a life of aimless trouble-making at home by the prospect of fame and plunder from the Crusades. It was perhaps the universal surge of response to the Crusades that helped to ensure their ultimate moral failure. Along with wealth and man-power they mobilised even greater resources of ambition and the cynical self-interest of adventurers who were anything but chivalrous or devout.

In St. Bernard's early manhood, however, the movement, still young and partly idealistic, did not lack warriors who held passionately that a holy war required holiness of life. The military orders were born of this conviction, and in 1120 St. Bernard, keenly alive to their value in society as well as to their spiritual potential, helped to draw up the Rule of one of the most famous of them. The Knights of the Temple, whose special function was to protect the Holy Places at Jerusalem and care for the pilgrims who flocked to them, were constituted on terms of close association and even submission to the Order of Cîteaux whose white habit they adapted to their military dress.

In his Letter to the Templars, *In Praise of the New Warfare* (1128), St. Bernard sums up the life of a Christian knight as an eager expectation of death:

> Whether they die in bed or in battle, the death of the saints is always precious in the sight of the Lord, but death on the battlefield is more precious just as it is more glorious. O the safety of a life lived in the purity of detachment! A life of safety indeed, for you look on death fearlessly, you long for it with all your heart, and you welcome it with devotion![5]

Their life meanwhile must combine the comfortlessness of active service (unrelieved by the hunting and hawking pastimes of their caste) with the celibate rigour of a monk's vocation. In contrast to the expensive frivolity of secular soldiers who rush to arms on any low impulse of rage or appetite,[6] the Templars, disciplined by a quasi-monastic obedience, strike terror into the enemies of the Holy City in the power of a righteous cause which may even justify the spilling of pagan blood. But their primary role as guardians and defenders cuts them off uncompromisingly from the professional killers of commonplace war. St. Bernard hesitated as to a name for the new breed, 'whether to call them monks or soldiers? To tell the truth both names are appropriate for they lack nothing, neither the gentleness of the monk nor the cool courage of the soldier. What can I say but that it is the Lord's doing and marvellous in our eyes!'[7]

Although he ordered his abbots to excommunicate any monks who abandoned their vocation to join the Crusade of 1146, St. Bernard laid no embargo on recruitment to the cloister from the ranks of chivalry. Monks had 'no need to sew the Cross on their clothes when they always carry it in their hearts, so long as they cherish their religious way of life',[8] but a soldier might honourably graduate from earthly to heavenly warfare by becoming a monk. Indeed, some years after St. Bernard's death, it became possible to do so even without abandoning the profession of arms. In 1158, during the struggle for the re-conquest of Spain from the Moors, members of the garrison at Calatrava joined the Cistercian Order under the Abbot of Fitero while remaining soldiers. Some thirty years later the Community was affiliated to Morimond, one of the four daughters of Cîteaux, and their incorporation into the order was confirmed by a papal bull in 1198. The warrior monk had become more than a figure of speech. Two ideals had fused to produce a new medieval type of holiness, 'the serjeant of Jesus Christ'. At least one such instance of the type is pregnant with suggestions for the *Quest of the Holy Grail*. About 1222, a Templar by the name of Nonus Artandus entered the Novitiate at Clairvaux, bringing with him relics from the Holy Land which included a fragment of the Cross and *a silver table*. The Red Cross knight turned monk is a ready-made sketch for Perceval.[9]

Meanwhile the eastward flow of expansion had brought the white monks bodily alongside the merchant traffic and the clashing armies of Islam and Christendom in what was just a further reach of their ubiquity. The early Cistercians had sought out wild and remote places for their hidden experiement in fidelity and solitude, but a hundred years later, by one of history's ironies, the unrivalled prestige of St. Bernard and his sons would guarantee their prominence in any sphere of Church or political affairs that called for spiritual leadership. Traces of this large influence are to be found all through the *Quest*; where, for example, a theological or moral issue is in question, it is almost always the Cistercian position that is adopted, and in such a way as to silence further argument.[10]

It is possible to regard the involvement of Cîteaux in temporal affairs as a trap into which the new Order was drawn unawares through its acquisition of the spectacular gifts and personality of St. Bernard. Alternatively, it was the inevitable process whereby a spiritual *corps d'élite* came to terms with its own epoch, losing in primitive zeal what it gained in effective power to influence the course of events. A third view, however, might see it as a positive if rather infirm witness to the sovereignty and glory of God as He works out His purpose in the confused affairs of sinful men. In the light of Christian revelation, the whipping up of passions which harden into the enmities of history, manifests the attempt of fallen spirits to harness to their own despairing struggle for dominion, in a world where time is running out, the impaired and mis-directed powers of a sick humanity. In such a light, a Cistercian monastery on the Mount of Transfiguration, a Cistercian abbot at the councils of the Crusades, is a sign of the hidden and humble engagement with evil that will go on until the last days at the contemplative heart of the Church. This unseen warfare, the clue to the riddle of monastic withdrawal in any age, is also a prominent theme in the *Quest*. Repeatedly, in its allegorical scenes, we are shown evil forced out of its strongholds and compelled to a self-declaration that ends in smoke and stench.

> Galahad waited no more but set out towards the tomb and as he drew near he heard a rending shriek as of a being in torment and a voice which cried: 'Stand back, Galahad, thou servant of Jesus Christ, and come not nigh to me, for thou wouldst yet oust me from the place where I have lodged to long'. But Galahad was undismayed and went up to the tomb, and as he bent forward to grasp the head he saw smoke and flame belch out followed at once by a thing most foul and hideous, shaped like a man. At this sight he blessed himself, knowing it for the evil one. At the same moment he heard a voice which said to him: 'Ah Galahad, most holy one, I see thee so girt about by angels that my power cannot endure against thee. I cede the place to thee.' At this Galahad again made the sign of the Cross and gave thanks to Our Lord. (p. 62)[11]

A full interpretation by one of the monks follows this Adventure of the Tomb, which, though personal to Galahad, is shown to have cosmic significance. In Christian tradition the same is true in principle of all resistance to evil, however trivial the occasion, for every rebuke in the Name of Christ releases the power of his redemptive judgement into the situation and opens it up to the grace of the Holy Spirit. Some understanding, however small, of this fundamental truth and of the purity of heart in which it must be held is necessary for a life of prayer that is Christian in the fullest sense, and a very great part of the training for such a life will consist of learning to recognize the demons for what they are in order to disarm them. It is for this that all knowledge of the self and of the surrounding world is to be received and endured; it is for this also that the intelligent Christian will submit to the guidance of one who has himself passed through the rigours of the spiritual combat. Ultimately, then, it is the warrior character of the Cistercians that qualifies them for their distinctive role in the *Quest*, a role of partnership in chivalric holiness that would have had St. Bernard's entire approval. The bold stroke which planted Cîteaux quickset in the sinister zone between Camelot and Corbenic, gave the author his dramatic occasion and his message its note of spiritual authority. With the *Quest of the Holy Grail*, the white monks enter the literature of the Middle Ages.

III

Between 1200 and 1230 an Arthurian Cycle in prose was written, probably by three French authors in collaboration. It begins with the earlier career of Lancelot and ends with the *Mort Artu* which tells of the final break-up of Arthur's kingdom. In between, and carefully linked with both, is the *Quest of the Holy Grail*, which is probably the work of a clerk in minor orders in close touch with Cistercian circles in France. Nothing more can be said with any certainty about the Author.[12] That odd flourish of anonymity with which he ends by ascribing his book to Walter Map, already fifteen years dead and no friend to the Cistercians, is in keeping with the gently ironic turn of mind by which some of his finest effects are achieved.

The Celtic roots of the Grail legend itself are buried in a ruinous landscape of pagan mythology where scholars are still digging for them to this day, and in the present essay, such arcane territory can be safely given a wide berth. The passage of a magic Horn of Plenty through Irish and Welsh legend by way of the Breton story-tellers into the sophisticated *Perceval* of Chrétien de Troyes (1180), is also bristling with complexities which need not be dwelt on here. But even in Chrétien's unfinished Romance, the Vessel and its attendant Lance, moving with mysterious autonomy up and down the Hall of the Fisher King, flicker with hints of an awful significance not yet disclosed to the imagination of the poet.

A transformation of the Grail went on among Chrétien's successors in what has been called 'an orgy of copy-catting',[13] until it emerged at last in a Christian light in a poem written in 1200 by Robert de Borron. Appealing to the apocyrphal evidence of *'un grand livre'*, which has never been identified, the poem tells how Joseph of Arimathaea sent from the Holy Land, in the care of Josephus his son, to the Vale of Avalon in Britain, the very dish in which Jesus consecrated the Bread and Wine of His Sacrifice at the Last Supper. It was, moreover, the same Vessel that received the Blood and Water as they flowed from the pierced side of Jesus on the Cross (and thus it came later to be explicity coupled with the Lance of Longinus which dealt that wound). Thereafter it was entrusted to a privileged line of Grail-Keepers, the Fisher Kings, who guarded it in the jealous seclusion of their Castle at Corbenic.

Here then is the Grail, a substantial Christian relic, venerated and prized as the holiest thing in Britain. All that it is and portends is now contingent on the Eucharist and the Passion, two of the most profound verities of the Christian faith. The magic properties of its pagan prototype, though never quite eliminated, dwindle—where they cannot be harmonised and hallowed—to a residue of folklore which, it must be confessed, keeps awkward company with the Vehicle of divine Mysteries that the Grail has now become. It was to all this that the Author of the *Quest* fell heir.

But he had something other to do than simply to continue or elaborate the story. Taking the raw materials available—a few famous Round Table knights, the well-tested popularity of an allegorical Romance organized round some great adventure—he would use the Holy Grail as a means of leading the conventional quest out of its finite mood into regions of the spirit from which (except in the case of Bors) there would be no return to Arthur's kingdom. He wrote his book principally neither to entertain nor even to instruct, but to steal the hearts of his readers to a new allegiance, to awaken with 'the cry of a heavenly chivalry' desires forgotten, overlaid or stifled in the absorbing service of Courtly Love. Such a purpose would require the overthrow, the calculated exposure of that very cult which, for all its beauty and persuasive power, held the spirit of its votaries in bondage to corruption.

If it was second nature for medieval readers to probe under the surface of any story for its hidden meaning on many levels, even so, some very special skills, some striking innovation would be needed to effect what amounts to a literary *conversio morum* in the two governing ideals of secular culture. The new element was already provided for in the overall structure of the Cycle, but its development is entirely the work of the *Quest*. In breadth and mobility of learning, as well as in spiritual temper and the organizing power of a great artist, the unknown Clerk would prove equal to his task.

IV

In less skilled hands the decision to put the Cistercians in charge of the Quest, supplanting knightly glamour with an austere militant holiness, imposing a monastic programme for conversion on some of the most wildly popular heroes of the age, might well have quenched the light of the Grail under a wet blanket of edification. Instead, only now does it begin to shed the unearthly radiance to which bodily eyes are blind, to address the appeal for which only the inmost spirit has an answer.

On the Eve of Pentecost, the Hermit Nascien arrives at Camelot to announce the Quest in terms which time and again will echo St. Paul's words (I Cor. 2:9): 'Eye hath not seen, ear hath not heard, neither have entered into the heart of man, the things which God hath prepared for them that love Him'. The Quest of the Holy Grail is opened to the whole chivalric world at that world's acknowledged centre, and in the challenge, a judgement, not harsh, but final, is passed upon all that sustains its dazzling existence.

It is 'the loud lament of the disconsolate chimera' that we hear in Arthur's reproaches, in Guinevere's distracted grief at the loss of Lancelot. All Camelot turns out in dismay to watch the King's chivalry ride out to the first elementary tests that will shortly thin its ranks to a handful of three. For though every knight kindles to the Quest as to the supreme challenge of his knighthood, its early stages will find almost the entire Round Table hopelessly unfit to pursue it on the conditions of conversion and renunciation laid down by Nascien. For 'the natural man receiveth not the things of the Spirit of God: for they are foolishness to him: neither can he know them because they are spiritually discerned.' Confidently bringing the experience of years to the enterprise, they find themselves foiled time and again by that for which none of it has prepared them. Like the White Knight they have had 'plenty of practice' and can do nothing but fall off.

From now on, though his penitence will take Lancelot a good part of the way, the Quest belongs properly only to the three knights from whom it is possible to look for a spiritual response to an adventure of the spirit. Each rider plunges separately into the darkness of the forest, hushed, thinly-peopled, alive with menace, but pricked here and there by 'the ironic points of light' which are the abbeys and hermitages of the White Monks. To these, the fixed and stable features in the landscape of errantry, the care and direction of the chosen knights has been assigned.

A definite presence is therefore the first Cistercian factor in the story. Of the ten abbeys visited by the knights, four are designated as abbeys of white monks; the rest, in the absence of other information, may well be the same. Of the fifteen hermits and recluses, one who wears the white habit is the centre of a thoroughly Cistercian episode.[14] It is a presence sparse and functional enough, perhaps, confined also to the early stages of the Quest, but here the Cistercians are exclusively charged with the authority of the *whole* Church. It is they who interpret the Quest, unravel the signs, expound the Scriptures, administer the Sacraments, entertain, exhort and scold the knights. As spiritual soldiers themselves, who keep watch in prayer and abstinence, who safeguard the doctrines of the Church, and 'put on the armour of Our Lord' to celebrate his Mysteries, they preside naturally over the fortunes of their lay counterparts. Even at Camelot the day is measured by the rhythm of the monastic Hours of prayer, but beyond its walls, the world itself is Cistercian and to venture there in light-minded ignorance of its values is to draw down confusion on all the faculties.

For on yet another level of meaning in a text whose symbolism has been well described as *'Multiple, stratifiée et polyvalente'*,[15] the Quest follows the pattern of monastic initiation. The first condition is to leave Camelot, to turn one's back on the grace of the fashion of the perishing world of Romance. The second is to embrace chastity, letting the image of one's Lady pale away before an exploit she is powerless either to inspire or to reward. The third is to give evidence of the will to convert, by 'entering at the gateway of cleanness, which is confession'. Something of the boyish ardour of St. Bernard and his thirty companions knocking at the door of Cîteaux lingers about the opening of the Quest.

Aspiration is followed by a novitiate in which vocation is put to the test. The essential thing her is to grasp the root of *obedientia*, to be willing to listen and to submit one's wounds for healing in the infirmary of conversion, in order to begin to move towards a clearer perception of what was undertaken in the first energy of enthusiasm. Though an almost mulish persistence will keep some of them blundering into dangers they are helpless to combat, the self-reliant, the careless and the evasive are left in no doubt that they are wasting their time. What excites praise and admiration at Camelot is shown up as hollow self-love by the quiet penetration of the hermits, whose long schooling in prayer and solitude has made them accurate readers of the human heart.

'Gawain, Gawain, you have betrayed me', cries Arthur, 'for no man can love another as I have loved you and that love is not new-born, but dates from the hour I first recognised the virtues lodged in you.' (p. 49) But, 'Gawain', a hermit tells him, 'it is a long time since you were knighted, and in all these years you have done little enough for your Maker. You are an old tree now, bare of leaves and fruit. Bear this in mind if nothing else, that Our Lord should have pith and bark since the enemy has had flowers and fruit.' (p. 173)

With faultless courtesy Gawain refuses his third opportunity to pass, by accepting the help offered him, from a nominal adherence to a living faith and so condemns himself to the futile round of those 'who are unable to hold to track or trail but wander footloose in outlandish parts' (p. 144). We meet his kind again in Henry Crawford of *Mansfield Park*; shallowness, 'want of principle' are as deadly disabilities in the eyes of Jane Austen as in those of a thirteenth-century hermit.

For the more biddable Lancelot, much more can be done. Convicted of sloth and presumption in the very presence of the Grail, he is stripped of his armour and left, like a punished monk,[16] outside the chapel where he has dozed inert. The lesson will have to be repeated when he is bundled out of the Chapel of the Grail for his impulsive disobedience, but before that he has to learn that his secret liaison with the Queen, for years, as he had believed, the motive power and inspiration behind his unparalleled carrer as a knight, has in fact cost him the integrity before God with which he had set out in life and which he will hardly, if ever, recover.

The effect of these home truths on Lancelot is a painful wrenching of his whole affective nature, which robs him of all joy in a world that until now has always smiled on his effortless pre-eminence. Nevertheless, he has the courage to persevere in penance, accepting the hair-shirt and a strict rule of confession, giving up meat and wine, and cheerfully sleeping under the stars without intermission of his prayer. 'No longer quite a layman', Lancelot makes a momentous break with the character and way of life which nearly a century of Romance had built up for him, and as long as he can depend on the conditions of the Quest and the watchful care of his monastic guides, he will be able to sustain his new life with more than ordinary zeal. Artistically, however, Lancelot's conversion in terms, alternately, of adventure and counsel achieves two things. It transposes the monastic ascesis in to a Romance setting at the same time as it disposes finally of the Romance ideal. It is that Lancelot who has always excelled his companions in the spurious poverty, chastity, and obedience exacted by the imperium of Love, who must now begin all over again to cultivate starved and neglected virtue in the soil of a broken heart. It is not too much to say that until this reversal of values has been demonstrated beyond all doubt—that is, until two-thirds of the tale is told—the Quest, rightly understood, cannot even begin. Only those who have survived the stunning impact of self-knowledge and are prepared to go forward on the same unflattering terms into the stage which corresponds in monastic life to Profession, in spiritual maturity to the contemplative life,[17] can entertain any hope of even recognizing 'adventures of a spiritual order'. As Perceval hears the words, 'Thou hast conquered and art healed; enter this ship and go wheresoever adventure leads thee', he commits himself 'with the greatest joy a man can know' to the winds that will unite him with Galahad and Bors. Lancelot, however, emerges from his trance at Corbenic to be no less plainly told, 'Sir knight, you can leave off the hair-shirt now for your quest is ended. There is no use your striving any longer to seek the Holy Grail for we know that you will not see any more of it than you have seen. May God now bring us those who are to see that more.' (p. 265)

V

From the outset the Author has never tired of insisting on the indescribable, the ineffable nature of 'that more' which is the reward of a realistic pursuit of the Quest. To describe its early stages, he has drawn on a rich iconography of flowers, colours, animals, and jewels, composing a landscape in which castles disappear into thin air, ruined chapels blaze with candlelight in the depths of the forest, 'strange isles in distant seas' provide the solitude in which the flesh is tried and the heart sounded, ships without crews are driven on the wind, demons disguised in the showy opulence of light women attack the chastity of the knights, and at every juncture the matter-of-fact monks and hermits, like policemen directing the traffic of the supernatural, present the challenge of unfuddled responsibility for the choices mirrored in the figments of Romance.

But how, when he crosses the wavering and uncertain boundary between the moral and the mystical life, when his knights begin to live 'in the Spirit', how then is he to fulfil without falsification or anti-climax the expectations raised in his readers? What images will evoke the unimaginable?

It will be of value here to consider once again the purpose which the basic materials of the *Quest* are to serve by comparing it with that of a contemporary work, the *Dialogue on Miracles* of Caesarius of Heisterbach.[18] In a number of cases the *Quest* makes use of stories which are told also by Caesarius and must therefore have been circulating in French and German monasteries of the time.

The *Dialogue*, protracted over some hundreds of pages, between a monk and a novice, is in essence a moral dissertation in the happy form of little cautionary tales, vignettes of sanctity, 'crumbs', Caesarius modestly calls them, which he has collected from the loaves of serious learning, in order that the record of signs and wonders, so well-attested from the early days of Cîteaux, may not be lost to posterity. These delightful miracle stories, which are first of all the credentials of Cîteaux to the Church, serve also the secondary purpose of instructing the young and dispelling doubts in matters of faith and morals by pointing to the often uncomfortable irruption of the supernatural into everyday life.

The *Quest* by contrast, occupying a far narrower canvas, has nothing to vindicate or defend. Rather, it makes use of the Cistercian order, as it makes use of Arthurian legend and Romance conventions, and even of the Scriptures themselves, to open up a prospect for the eyes of the spirit, offering the reader through the most sublime images that memory can command, such glimpses of eternity as the submission of art and learning to faith will afford him. Nowhere is the difference in spiritual atmosphere more palpable than in the climactic liturgical scenes at Corbenic and Sarras.

In the section of the *Dialogue* on the Sacrament of the Body and Blood of Christ, Caesarius is entirely concerned with the transubstantiation of the eucharistic species, amassing evidence in the form of blood-stained corporals, pieces of raw flesh found in the ciborium, and the punishments visited on profanity of any kind. The more or less crude appeal of the evidence is directly to the senses, and at times to the animal fear which such evidence can excite.

The appeal of the *Quest*, on the other hand, is *through* the charged, doctrinal symbolism of the Church, to the heart, the seat and organ of rational love in its desire to see and to know. At Corbenic, certainly, Josephus, like the priests in the *Dialogue*, elevates a host, which in his hands takes the form of a fiery Child; but this is no more than a stage in an ascent which develops apocalyptically: 'in the darkness of the body and the soul's light'. When the Lord steps naked and bleeding out of the Holy Grail and greets the companions with words of love and praise, it is, He admits, because they have sought Him 'so diligently that I can hide Myself from you no longer'. It is the perfection of their faith that compels the disclosure of a divine presence that has never been in doubt.

Before this penultimate climax of the *Quest*, the mind's eye has ranged through Christendom to capture for the scene the most luminous traits of

Christian art. The Divine Liturgy, in which angels carrying the instruments of the Passion minister to Christ the High Priest at the heavenly altar, was a favourite theme for decoration in the domes of Byzantine Churches. Something not unlike it, with saints instead of angels, is described by Caesarius in the Vision of the Holy Maid of Quida at Candlemas. The Communion of the Apostles,[19] another motif characteristic in the East but unknown in western Europe, may have come to the Author's knowledge as a result of the Crusades; while in Lancelot's more partial experience of the mystery, the suggestion of an anthropomorphized Trinity recalls, for example, Caesarius's account[20] of a Dove hovering over the chalice and paten and, more generally, the visions granted to many devoutly expectant people in that age.[21]

But what these exalted scenes suggest to the imagination is something with which perhaps children are most of all familiar. It is that experience of being caught up into the ambit of one's contemplation; or, it might be, the moment at which the statue comes alive, the portrait, in answer to a mute appeal, steps out of its frame and enters into warm and vital relations with the beholder. In the material world this may never quite happen: at Corbenic, the Court of Heavenly Love, it really does. The icons venerated in a thousand churches are stirred to life and activity in the presence of true worship. The angels swing their censers, they tilt the Lance, so that the Blood of a Sacrifice perpetually pleaded drips into the Holy Grail. The Chapel seems to take on the dimensions of a vast basilica, as it might be at Venice or Constantinople, wing-swept, filled with light and drifting fragrance. As he gives the Kiss of Peace to Galahad, Josephus makes him participant as deacon in the rite that is, and is not, a liturgical celebration;[22] and the knights are drawn into the interchanges of love and knowledge which are the uninterrupted life of Heaven. Christ the Pelican of Mercy walks to them out of the Grail, not in high priestly vestments but in the veiled glory of his suffering Humanity, to give Himself with his own hands to his friends. The grace of the Eucharistic banquet is, as He reminds them, offered freely to all men, good and bad alike; but to see the Saviour *apertément*, in the sense of being admitted to a supra-rational knowledge of the Crucified as the Wisdom of God and the Power of God, requires all the purity of heart which He commends in them. The intellectual vision of a white Hart passing through the window panes of a little woodland oratory, found in them the response of an enlightened faith which has led directly to the living presence of 'Our Lord Jesus Christ,

Himself the greatest and most wonderful of Sacraments'.[23] 'Long looking, long loving, long desiring, these win at last to the inmost being of a thing.'[24] These, unexhausted even in fulfilment and patient of further testings still to come, have worn the veil of separation to a thinness which only death can now dissolve. 'They have attained', He tells them, 'to the spiritual life whilst still in the flesh.' 'Their faces are wet with tears of awe and love.' (p. 276)

VI

It should be no surprise to find a thirteenth century Clerk moving with as much ease in the forests of Biblical allegory as in the cultivated garden of Courtly Love. In the mind of this book we have discovered also a deeply sacramental source of imagery, and will have presently to reckon with a degree of saturation in Cistercian thought that cannot be measured by the tally of neat textual correspondences. In the later stages of the Quest, where conflict is subdued to expectation, the hermits close their doors, the monks are silent. A thunderbolt of divine exasperation rescues Bors and sobers Lionel into shamefaced uncertainty. In the comparative calm and clarity that follow, the eye is free to catch the gleams of meaning that play like sunlight on leaves, the ear to pick up echoes started on every page. When homily and exhortation have done their work, Cistercianism remains in the very air breathed by the companions as Solomon's Ship carries them unstriving towards the term of their Quest.

It would be a misuse of delight systematically to unplait the strands of allegory into which the *Quest* is woven, for its coherence and depth both reside in the interplay of images which will not be restricted to one or even two or three meanings. Nevertheless, a deeper access into the mind of the Author may perhaps be gained by a closer scrutiny of what, amidst such a profusion of sources, is most intimately and singularly his own. The Quest, the Holy Grail, Galahad, these three interpret one another; but Galahad was made for nothing but to go upon the Quest, and the Holy Grail delivers its ultimate secret to no one but Galahad.[25]

The perfect knight, 'he who stands so grounded in the love of Christ that no adventure can tempt him into sin', cannot be understood—or liked—except from within an eschatological perspective; which is to say that only from the far side of the Quest do the fully human proportions of

Galahad reveal themselves.

In the 'novitiate' stage, where false knights are unhorsed and damsels delivered with almost cowboy predictability whenever he appears, not even the hints and prophecies of the hermits provide the real clue to his personal destiny. There his sovereign ease of conquest and freedom from moral struggle simply indicate the advance position from which, in his case, the Quest begins. He is alone and chooses to be alone, not out of wilfulness but because there is no one to keep up with him. Until there is, he will be exercised at full stretch in preliminary works of obedience, which bear an analogy to the messianic signs of Christ in relation to the supreme 'work' of his Passion.

Charles Williams conceived Galahad as pure allegory, as 'only that in the human soul which finds Christ'.[26] If this were so, what of Perceval, Bors, and Lancelot who also find Him? More truly, Galahad is the *whole* man in search of God, and it is precisely that disconcerting wholeness that baffles the natural mind. If the Land of Unlikeness is to be reckoned the normal habitat of rational man, then certainly Galahad will seem to be a perverse anomaly; though even there, the least percipient of his fellows recognize in his beauty and valour something after which their hearts hanker, so that their chief object is to catch up with him and pursue the Quest at his side.

Galahad has 'put on the Lord Jesus Christ, making no provision for the flesh'. His messianic role, his likeness to Christ 'in semblance only and not in sublimity', though as daring conceptions as any in medieval literature, are based on nothing less firm and ultimate than Scripture itself. In Christ, Galahad is a 'new creation'; he fulfils the promise to the disciples, 'Greater things than these shall ye do', and the strength in which he continues the work of Redemption is that of the promised indwelling of the Holy Spirit in the hearts of the obedient. In short, he has appropriated his baptismal inheritance with the deliberation and energy of a will not yet sapped by the delusions of self-love, and fortified with every fresh choice of reality. The pentecostal scarlet and white in which he arrives at Camelot, his red armour, his escort of angels, and the great images that surround his adventures—the Shield, the Sword, the Ship—are not so much the privileges reserved to heaven's favourite as the insignia of an integral fidelity, an unwavering love and resolution.

Faith, Chastity, Desire—it is these that set Galahad apart from the other knights. Where unrepented evil-living has closed and hardened them against the Holy Spirit, Galahad's body is the enclosure of a total consecration in which he addresses himself to the task of his short life. Chastity in him is far more than carnal ignorance; rather it is the measure of his unwasted powers of loving, which overflow in compassion and radiant good manners; just as his feats of arms are the measure of his faith, and the great Red Cross Shield its luminous symbol.

Throughout the Quest, the sign of the Cross—the little confession of faith 'in which a knight should place his greatest trust'—punctuates each pause for decision, each lifting of the heart in prayer; and it is the self-confidence that preens just below the surface of a modest and manly bearing that is punished and condemned as faithlessness itself. 'O man of little faith and most infirm belief! . . . You thought your prowess would see you through but reason played you false, for the words referred to a spiritual order while you see only the temporal . . .'[27] The knights of the Round Table are under judgement because, almost to a man, they have nothing to show for their solemn profession of chivalry but an ephemeral prestige, the pride of life, and the shadow of a great name among men as faithless as themselves.

The marvellous Ship, then, inscribed all round with unnerving prohibitions for those whose faith falls short, cannot be taken for the Church, the Ark of refuge for sinners. This Ship offers safe-conduct only to those whose faith is the proven mainspring of all their actions. The rest it can only reject, for 'I am naught but faith and true belief'. The first voyage in the Ship resembles the transition from novitiate to profession. Here Galahad completes his armour; he takes the Sword of the Spirit, and is girded by Perceval's virgin sister with the belt woven from her own hair.[28] In this second investiture, Galahad provides also a re-definition of knighthood in accordance with the spiritual ideals of St. Bernard. It is the same man who 'in his lifetime shall exemplify the sum of earthly chivalry' who will shortly come to 'live wholly in the Spirit'. The spiritual man and the true knight are one thing. The vow to go upon the Quest, which Gawain is the first to take and which Galahad silently embodies, turns out to have the character of the vows of Profession which, enshrining a relationship sealed within a state of life, rather than prescribing a task, look not towards fulfilment but consummation. The Holy Grail is not something for the cleverest and strongest to clutch as a prize; passionately as it is sought, it moves, it comes and goes at its pleasure. The work of the Quest is at every stage, so to cleanse the perceptions that they may be awake to the presence of the holy Vessel. It is a vigil which Galahad never relaxes, even in sleep.

Is there something inhuman and repellent about the Hero of the Quest? Only, perhaps, by the standards of the modern psychological novel, which can be applied in happy disregard of the Dominical command, 'Be ye therefore perfect'. Pauphilet warns us against finding Lancelot more attractive just because he is worse, *'pénitent perpetual'*, always sliding back along the lines of human attachment. The text is most careful to show that Lancelot had the same start in life as his son. He need have forfeited nothing, with perseverance he might have recovered much of what he lost, but old custom has made the life of the passions too sweet and strong to abandon. Whereas Lancelot will go back to pleasure the Queen and deepen himself in perfidy to his liegelord, 'perfection' in Galahad has meant such a progressive strengthening of his original endowment that, although he remains as capable of sin as any free-willed member of the race, the confirmed disposition to choose God in everything has made him virtually proof against sin's infection. So while Lancelot enjoys his company for a time, only Perceval and Bors gain that stability of like-mindedness that makes them so welcome to Galahad that the three, meeting at last on board, burst into the unmotivated laughter of sheer delight in being together.

Laughter and tears, the two gifts which come unbidden from the hidden springs of a common humanity, far from being excluded from the high places of the spirit find in the 'clear eternal weather' their purest and freest expression.

> We had fed the heart on fantasies,
> The heart's grown brutal from the fare

said Yeats of his fellow Irishmen in 'a time of Civil War'. By the same token, Grace, the food of reality constantly assimilated, has expanded Galahad's heart to the full capacities of a human being, a man and a lover. On the second voyage, Perceval, overhearing his repeated prayer for death, asks him what he means by it; and Galahad confides to him the beatitude of his vision at Corbenic where he had seen

> so great a host of angels and such a multitude of heavenly beings, that I was translated in that moment from the earthly plane to the celestial, to the joy of the glorious martyrs and the beloved of Our Lord. And because I hope to be again as favourably placed as I was then, or better

still to contemplate this bliss, therefore I made the plea you overheard. And thus I trust that I shall depart this life by God's goodwill while looking on the glories of the Holy Grail. (p. 280)

This echo from Hebrews (12:22-25) should dispel misgivings about Galahad's ruthless solitude. The enigmatic knight who gives everyone the slip, opens his arms wide to welcome his true companions in the spirit. The love between Perceval and Galahad 'ran deep'. 'I longed for your presence, now I joy in it', he tells Bors; and 'Oh that they could all come with me!' he cries at Corbenic, where his all but final vision is of an enormous crowd he asks nothing better than to join.

VII

Galahad reaches his full *human* stature in response to a *divine* love; so much (in a clear reflection of Ephesians 3:14-20) is evident from his development in the story. But the very fact that this happens can lead us to discover further debts to the rich doctrinal resources of the Cistercian Fathers.

While it would be merely captious to belittle St. Bernard's influence in a work so clearly inspired by his personality and ideals, and so redolent of his mysticism, there is nevertheless at least one weighty reason to look for some of its cardinal ideas to an even more profound thinker of the Cistercian school, William of St. Thierry.[29]

What is well known today, namely that St. Bernard and William differ in their conception of the origin and growth of love in the soul, can hardly have been evident in the early thirteenth century when those of William's works which were not neglected or unknown were attributed to St. Bernard himself. But to read the *Quest* as strictly as possible in the light of its own times, is to be made aware that it is launched from ideas foreign to St. Bernard's thought and intrinsic to that of William. Having fastened on this clue at the outset, it is hard indeed not to see the Quest unfolding all the way in harmony with William's teaching as modern scholarship has taught us to value and understand it. To follow this thread as far as it will go will not be to shoulder St. Bernard aside, but rather to acclaim in the wisdom of Cîteaux a range, a depth, a diversity of gifts, which—nourished as they all are on the Bible, the Liturgy, and the Fathers—have been expressed in voices that are, at the same time, distinctively personal and resonant with the thoughts of other men. The freedom to explore, conferred by a writer who acknowledges no sources other than the Bible, will not be abused by such a rapid and fumbling exposure of the *Quest* to William's thought as may be attempted here, if in the end it should be found to shed some light on them both.

Frequently in his writings, William seems to hark back to a famous passage in the *Confessions* of St. Augustine which is so striking an evocation of the hero of the *Quest* that it may be quoted at some length:

> A body inclines by its own weight to the place that is fitting for it. Weight does not always tend towards the lowest place, but the one which suits it best, for though a stone falls, flame rises. When things are displaced, they are always on the move until they come to rest in the place where they are meant to be. In my case, love is the weight by which I act. To whatever place I go I am drawn to it by love. By your Gift, the Holy Ghost, we are set aflame and borne aloft, and the fire within us carries us upward. Our hearts are set on an upward journey as we sing the Song of Ascents. It is your fire, your good fire, that sets us aflame and carries us upward. For our journey leads us upward to the heavenly Jerusalem. There if our will is good, You will find room for us, so that we shall wish for nothing else but to remain in Your House forever. (Book XIII)[30]

When William begins his treatise *On the Nature and Dignity of Love*[31] by saying, 'Love is a power which carries the soul by a natural inclination[32] to its destination', it is the idea of *naturalness* that gives him his starting point. The really important thing about man is the inalienability of his likeness to God, which however overlaid and disfigured by sin can never be entirely lost. Moreover, the damage can be made good; the sickness in the will can be healed; the sanity proper to the whole man can begin to be recovered as his normal condition as soon as he resumes, by a free choice, his progress towards nothing less than deification, 'union with God in the midst of the Trinity'.[33]

Given the normality of this 'kindly enclyning' of man 'to his kindly stede', the return need not be by way of human attachments successively transcended. It can be direct, by way of response to the Holy Spirit whose gifts of grace are already sown in the heart as seed that waits only to be cultivated. Still less can the return be by way of fleshly appetite. In the opening chapter of the same treatise, William denounces Ovid (the classical progenitor of the Courtly ideal) as the arch-corrupter of the *natural* affections of the heart. Nearly a century later, the *Quest* makes a radical break with the uncovenanted sexual love celebrated in the Romances as 'the fountain and origin of all good things'.[34] Thus the insistent emphasis on chastity in its primary sense is perhaps aimed at unmasking a deception practised upon the heart by 'the corrupt masters of fleshly love' even more than at imposing an iron law of conduct.

Now because the heart's *natural* desire never changes, is never superseded or outgrown, but remains from its first waking to its final consummation, God and nothing less than God, the means for attaining it must be those which God Himself has provided. Restoration must begin from the original design laid out in its buried foundations. In *The Mirror of Faith*, William teaches that this design, the hallmark of man's relationship with the Blessed Trinity, can be restored in the exercise of the little trinity of virtues—faith, hope, and charity—implanted in the soul new-born in Christ as the free gift of God, the strengths in which it is moved to respond to their source in the Holy Spirit and with his grace to recover the true likeness in which it was made.[35]

Since, therefore, the upward movement of the heart's return must involve it in resistance to all the downward drags of its disordered nature, the awakened soul will find itself doing battle on three fronts: with the appetites of its flesh, with the claims of the world that is passing away, and with the demons whose ambition is to bind man to his fallen condition and confirm him in deformity. The spearhead of this resistance is faith. Though the unity of gifts is interdependent—'each is in all and all is in each'—they are substantially one,[36] yet faith has a certain primacy because it initiates the movement of return and invites obedience at every stage. 'We experience charity first as faith and we begin to love and hope for only that in which we believe', but 'the soul, despite its natural bent towards God does not know how to return to its origin. And so, having neglected nature's teaching, it must needs have a man to instruct it in the search for happiness.'[37] Thus, when the soul is recalled to itself by a faint recollection of its original happiness—something that belongs almost to daily experience—'faith comes with its help and with the offer to set free the will'[38] to make choices in harmony with its deepest desires. In this way, the slow healing of the will begins.

The act of obedience is a concord of faith, hope, and love in submission to revealed truth and to the authority of those who can interpret it. Obedience is the will's first venture into the unknown, the Waste Forest where all the armour of the fleshly mind is worse than useless. Without this initial act of blind submission by which the heart opens itself to the only light and power that can help it, there is no future in the Quest of the Holy Grail. Faith will be arrested at the level of loveless assent where its influence on the direction of a human life must remain at a minimum, while a faithless persistence in the Quest misconceived—in a word, presumption—will lead not only to frustration and failure but to mortal sin.

Thus as the 'kindly enclyning' of the soul can well afford to bypass the experiences offered to *cupiditas*, so the awakened gift of faith can and indeed must be allowed to bypass the processes of discursive reasoning which can only lead the soul into deeper confusion and unlikeness. For, although reason will indeed find its proper exercise and its final fruition in exploring the truths revealed by faith, it can never by itself arrive at what is a pure gift. 'You cannot *conquer* the truth by the exercise of reason', says William. 'Truth is offered, the prize is given where there is no meriting.'[39] But by remaining open to receive everything from the grace of the Holy Spirit, the will, whose obedience began as a blind plunge of faith, passes into an obedience of predilection, for the love that is allowed to penetrate and suffuse the will deepens faith into understanding and tends to 'place all our desire in that rest which we shall find at the end of our pilgrimage'.[40]

It is only when the reign of the theological virtues is firmly established that reason may rightly resume its role and 'knock at the door of faith'[41] by humble reflection on the truths with which faith presents it. This is the continual recollection practised by the knights and seen at work most vividly in the humble, searching reverence with which the Quest is pursued by Bors. His profound sense of the insufficiency of the flesh to penetrate the Mystery of God in the Sacrament of the Eucharist, and his adoring confession of faith before it, are directly rewarded by the open vision for which he longs, when he is admitted at Corbenic to the 'sacred realities hidden from the sight of reason towards which the spirit of man is guided by the Holy Spirit in Person'.[42]

The theology of William of St. Thierry is like a shaft of light playing on the dynamic depths of faith and on the delicate transitions from blind assent to enlightened understanding, to knowledge in the spirit and finally, for the few, to the wisdom in which knowledge and love are inseparable—each, and at every stage, requiring a deeper surrender and effecting a more complete liberation of the will in its obedience. For these transitions correspond to subtle transformations in the whole man, which are analysed by William in his later works[43] with such power and precision as to constitute in the eyes of Cistercian scholars his most original contribution to ascetic and mystical theology. Here it must suffice simply to offer the belief that in the knights of the *Quest* we have the Romantic correlatives of those types of 'man-in-search-of-God' which William has discerned in the various stages of monastic and eremitic life. Lancelot, seeking God as the 'animal man', in the sense of a man still governed by the sensual and soulish aspects of his nature, never quite manages to pass beyond them into the 'rational life' of an enlightened delight in God. His love and humility—real as far as they go—remain at the 'animal' level, and the Quest concludes for him in the ecstatic swoon which is the limit of his capacity. Perceval, in the strength of his simplicity and constant love, and Bors by his passionate fidelity to truth, enter into the freedom of a life in which all their affections are assumed to the internal structure of the theological virtues, 'as the flesh cleaves to the bones'. 'Perfection here below', says William, 'is simply a complete forgetfulness of the past brought about by faith, hope and charity.'[44] This is beautifully evoked in the simplicity with which Galahad, at Perceval's suggestion, goes to sleep in Solomon's Bed. A single statement of fact takes the weight of an almost infinite allusiveness.

Galahad's sleep, 'long and deep' is God's gift to His beloved. But it is the sleep of a wakeful heart, like that of the Lord in the fishing-boat. The posts of his bed, carved from the Paradise Tree, are white, emerald green, and scarlet—like the purity, the patience, and the sacrifice of Christ. So Galahad sleeps under the shadow of Christ, as He slept on the beams of the Cross. He is supported in the frame of the theological virtues, the sheer white of faith, the steadfast green of hope, and charity, the colour of 'the rose with the tint of fire'. His faculties are not suspended in an ecstacy like that of Lancelot, but surrendered, in the sleep of 'complete forgetfulness of the past', to the divine Pilot of the Ship which is 'naught but faith'; '. . . and when he awoke, he looked ahead and beheld the city of Sarras.'

Here is the vestigial likeness common to all men, and re-established in the baptismal imprint, recovered in its fullness; not by conquest, but by surrender to the love of God, 'which moves over the love of faithful hearts drawing it to Himself through the natural inclination to cleave upwards to

Him like fire'.[45] When the obedient will has exceeded its own function, 'become something more than will; love, dilection, charity, unity of spirit, man is made one with the Spirit of God, not only with the unity which comes from willing the same thing, but the inability to will anything else'.[46]

Galahad is the chivalric portrait of the 'spiritual man', the man in whom the Holy Spirit's dominion is so unfettered that all the created gifts of nature and grace have become assimilated to the uncreated Charity Himself. 'When he [Galahad] shall live wholly in the Spirit', a hermit had told Lancelot, 'then he will slough off the garment of the flesh and join the company of the knights of Heaven.' It is no static, standardized perfection. It is all the way a growth, a process of becoming, a change from glory to glory, but one in which the intervals of hesitation between hearing and responding are so slight as to be imperceptible. The ascending movement of the Quest, impelled not by the thrust of sublimated energies but by a turning of the face in faith, hope, and love to meet a smile of heavenly encouragement, is maintained by the heart's willingness to receive everything as a gift from the Father, to claim nothing apart from Him, 'until it can show to the countenance of Grace its own face made pure again'.[47] This is the response of the 'intelligent heart' which is the whole secret of Galahad.

Nor is the phrase 'live wholly in the Spirit' a vague figure of speech, but precisely that condition towards which the knights are moving as they grow in aptitude for the revelations of the Holy Grail. The theology of the *Quest*, like that of William of St. Thierry, is Spirit-filled, Spirit-dominated, because it is He alone who initiates, presides over, and brings it to completion.

> Men may teach how to seek God and angels how to adore Him, but He alone teaches how to find Him, possess Him and enjoy Him. He Himself is the anxious quest of the man who truly seeks, He is the devotion of the man who adores in spirit and in truth, He is the wisdom of the man who finds, the love of him who possesses, the gladness of him who enjoys.[48]

It is not only in the key passages which clearly recall Pentecost that this primacy of the Spirit is affirmed; on page after page, under the figures of wind and flame and water, in the sunbeam that pierces the Hall at Camelot, the flash of a scarlet sleeve, the breeze that plays in Perceval's hair after his ordeal with the dragon, we divine the presence of the

> *Consolator optime,*
> *Dulcis hospes animae,*
> *Dulce refrigerium.*

At the same time that the *Quest* was being written, the great sequence, *Veni Sancte Spiritus*, of Archbishop Stephen Langton was gaining the hold on the hearts of the faithful which it retains to this day.[49] The *Quest* is so strewn with verbal traces of that mighty invocation of a divine Companion who, at every moment sustains and fills the solitude through which men *must* pass to the recovery of the fellowship which is his Gift that, in this context, it is itself the 'Song of Ascents', the measure and melody of Grace, at once urgent and serene, to which the knights travel 'in the darkness of the body and the soul's light'.

Indeed, for all its haughty-seeming individualism, its narrow intensity of focus, there is in this medieval Romance of the spirit an *ampleur* of allusion, which makes it a household treasure of all Christendom. The echoes are sent not only backwards but forward also into the future. The texts from which St. Thomas will compose the Office for the Feast of Corpus Christi seem to be waiting for him at the table of the Holy Grail. In nineteenth century Russia, St. Seraphim of Sarov will begin his teaching on the Holy Spirit in words that are identical in the mouths of Perceval's Visitor and the hermits of the Waste Forest;[50] and the mystical theology of a twelfth century master of synthesis has ensured that while the thought worlds of East and West would continue to drift apart, doctrines wrought out by the Greek Fathers should set a course for the crowning adventure of King Arthur's knights.

At the same time, having seen just a little of what is yielded by the laminated symbols that enfold the figure of a sleeping knight, we should be warned against too precise definitions, too confident ascriptions of meaning in anything that touches a mystery to which no one holds all the clues. So often, in order to understand more deeply, it is not a question of analysing but of looking. The Holy Grail itself asks ultimately for no other response. Unmistakeably and explicitly the symbol of the Grace of the Holy Ghost, it retains to the end an intrinsic reality that is all its own. 'You cannot conquer the truth'; you cannot imprison the Holy Grail in the nets of concept and definition. In a wonderfully suggestive phrase, William of St. Thierry says that 'the soul is poured into the receptacle of its desires'.[51] The Holy Grail, whatever else besides, is certainly a receptacle. It ministers to the shallow cravings even of the hard-hearted and unperceiving; it is the Vehicle of all sacramental grace in food and drink, healing and renewal of life; and it discloses to the eye of faith the secret of the divine Presence in the Sacrament of the altar. For the knights whose thirst for God is insatiable, it is that which focusses their expectation of *all* that God has in store for those who love him: vision, knowledge, homecoming to the Land of Likeness, union of the Triune Godhead in love with his creature, the whole torrent of his generosity poured out in beatitude.

After Corbenic, the Grail stays with the three companions on its silver table. It sails with them to Sarras where it sustains and refreshes them in prison. When Galahad has endured the year of kingship required of him, it resumes for the last time its Eucharistic function in the basilica at Sarras. Once more it is Josephus who presides, but this time over a scene that is significantly bare of all the symbolic richness of the earlier revelations. He intones the Mass of the glorious Mother of God and as he approaches the Canon,[52] summons Galahad to look into the Holy Grail. He does so and is seized with violent trembling . . .

But then, how quietly, how temperately Galahad speaks of this moment for which his whole short life has been a preparation! It is as if the Grail at last has nothing to show him more limpid, more crystalline than a waterfall. 'Here is the springhead of endeavour. Here is the source of valour undismayed.' Not a stammering avowal, not a rapt silence, but the soft wonder of recognition. And in the prayer he now makes 'to pass in this state from earthly life to life eternal', there is a declaration of the Quest achieved. Once in a dream, Hector had seen Lancelot trying repeatedly to drink from a spring, surpassingly clear, which as often withdrew itself from his lips, until at last 'he must go back the way he came', for the Grace of God does not join itself with those who relish earthly things. But the soul of Galahad, athirst for the living God, is poured into the receptacle of its desires.[53]

When he has received the Sacrament there is nothing left for him to do but to leave his body on the flags of the basilica. But as for the last time he takes leave of his companions with the Kiss of Peace, he does so, turning to Bors, with the cordial simplicity and high touching grace which, here at least, Malory was to surpass the French writer in expressing: 'Fair Lord, salute me to Sir Lancelot my father and as soon as you see him, bid him be mindful of this unstable world'.

* * * * * * * * *

The 'Vulgate Cycle' has been likened to a cathedral whose spire is the *Quest*. The comparison is apt and useful, not least because the collaborating authors, like cathedral builders, were forced into acts of originality by the sheer spiritual height of their vision: a vision which must be realized, whether in stone or prose, within the limits set by a stern economy of means.

Great skill in handling the Matter of Britain was needed in order to ensure that the son of destiny begotten by Lancelot, hoodwinked in the thick darkness of the chamber at Corbenic, should answer in all respects to established Arthurian tradition. At the same time, the transcendent character of his mission required the support of theological truth on the one hand and human credibility on the other which the Cistercian Order was pre-eminently fitted to provide. For more than a hundred years it had embodied throughout Western Europe the dictum of Evagrius: 'He who prays according to truth is a theologian, a theologian is one who prays according to truth'. Even at this period of incipient decline, when it was about to be eclipsed by the rising star of the mendicant orders, the names of Bernard, Isaac, Gilbert, Aelred were still bywords for visible human holiness, realized in a way of life that rejected all half-measures and never ceased to importune men with the promises of the Gospel.

Such is the outline of the Quest, rising from the pleasant places of high medieval culture and soaring above them, hard as a diamond, narrow as a needle's eye, to the vanishing-point at which Galahad and the Grail together pass beyond the temporal order. But crowding into it and catching fire and brilliance from its perfect symmetry are the forms and images enlisted by a frugal prose to scatter in prismatic colours the insupportable singleness of the Light that streams from the Holy Grail. It is an achievement perhaps best acknowledged in words borrowed from the text itself. Lost in admiration of the Ship she has built, Solomon tells his wife: 'You have done a marvellous work. For if all earth's inhabitants were here, they would not be able to spell out the meaning of this Ship unless Our Lord revealed it to them, not do you understand it yourself for all you have built it.' (p. 234)

NOTES

1. All page numbers refer to *The Quest of the Holy Grail*, Penguin Classics edition, 1969. It was from this admirable translation by P.M.Matarasso that I first learned of the Cistercian background to the *Quest*, and my debt to it will be evident throughout this essay.

2. *The Making of the Middle Ages*, 1953, p. 246.

3. Caesarius of Heisterbach: *Dialogue on Miracles* translated in 2 vols. by H.von E. Scott and S. Bland. Routledge 1929. Book IV, ch. 3.

4. C.S. Lewis: *The Allegory of Love*. Oxford 1936, p. 23.

5. St. Bernard: *A la Louange de la Milice Nouvelle*, trans. E. de Solms, 1957, p. 54.

6. Lionel's murderous attack on his brother probably reflects the irrational behaviour of those knights who degraded the chivalric idea. (p. 205)

7. op. cit. p. 164.

8. *Letters of St. Bernard*, trans. Bruno Scott James, 1953. Letter 396, To His Brother Abbots.

9. For all background information about the role of Cîteaux in the medieval Church, and especially the Crusades, see A. Pauphilet: *Etudes sur la Quête del Saint Graal* (1923), an indispensable work.

10. This is conveyed as much by an atmosphere of authority reflecting the real prestige enjoyed by the Order as moral and doctrinal arbitrators as by direct references. But the prolonged controversy about taking the life of one's enemies and the degree of punishment due to heretics, which St. Bernard pronounces upon in his Letter to the Templars, is echoed in the *Quest*. 'Do not imagine that the adventures now afoot consist in the slaying of men or the murder of knights . . .' Galahad is careful to avoid doing serious injury to anyone until the incident at Count Ernol's castle leads to a massacre of the inmates, and his misgivings have to be allayed by a priest who assures him that the heinousness of their crimes demanded in justice the punishment of death. There is also the discussion about Grace and free will in which a hermit corrects Bors with a direct quotation from St. Bernard's treatise: 'For a man's good works proceed from the grace and guidance of the Holy Ghost, the evil from the enemy's seduction'. (p. 178) Gilson comments that it is never a good idea to argue a doctrinal point with a thirteenth century hermit. See op. cit. note 24.

11. This passage has a quite intrinsic value as a classic illustration of an exorcism,

but the account is dramatically foreshortened inasmuch as Galahad's virtue is such that his mere presence is enough to expel the infesting evil. His sign of the Cross places the whole incident under the mercy of God and acknowledges the victory as His with instant thanksgiving. The angels always attendant upon Chastity are visible to the demon. Cf. *Comus*, 1.1, 453-456 et seq.

> So dear to Heaven is saintly chastity,
> That when a soul is found sincerely so,
> A thousand liveried angels lackey her,
> Driving far off each thing of sin and guilt . . .

12. For a detailed study of sources and authorship, see R.S. Loomis: *Arthurian Literature in the Middle Ages, a Collaborative Symposium*, Oxford 1959; esp. chapters on the 'Origin of the Grail Legend', 'The Work of Robert de Borron', and 'The Vulgate Cycle'.

13. 'une véritable gloutonnerie de poncif', *Lumière du Graal*, ed. R. Nelli, 1951.

14. See pp. 137-139. An incident involving the hair-shirt worn by Cistercians and a sample of demonic trickery, typical of the stories told by Caesarius.

15. M. Lot-Borodine, op. cit. note 24.

16. Cf. Rule of St. Benedict, ch. 25, 'Of Graver Faults'.

17. This is not to imply that monastic Profession and the contemplative life are simultaneous, far less that they are synonymous, but simply to indicate that parallels exist at all levels of interpretation to which the *Quest* lends itself.

18. op. cit., note 3, Book VIII, ch. 20.

19. The introduction of nine quite unknown knights to make up the Apostolic number, though unsuccessful as a device for enriching the total event at Corbenic, shows the importance of the theme for the Author, who was determined that it should appear in his most ambitious scene. It is also these purely functional characters who elicit Galahad's cry, 'O that they could all come with me!'

20. op. cit. note 3, Book IX, ch. 29.

21. e.g. the Vision which Abbot Ralph of Fountains had of the Trinity during Lauds. See D. Knowles: *The Monastic Order in England*, Cambridge 1940, ch. 20, p. 357.

22. The language used of this Eucharistic rite is comparative rather than indicative. 'Josephus acted *as though he were entering* upon the Consecration of the

Mass. . . .' 'Having discharged the functions of a priest *as it might be* at the Office of the Mass . . .' (p. 275). The stress is not so much on the transubstantiation effected by the priest's action, as on a presence itself so overwhelming as, in this context, to eliminate the need for a liturgical consecration. It is the Word of God Himself Who comes out of the Grail—and with an immediacy infinitely more compelling than that of the Child in the Host. The eucharistic action is even more strikingly superseded in the scene at Sarras, when Galahad's final admission to the secrets of the Grail takes place immediately after the Offertory. 'When he came to the solemn part of the Mass and *had taken the paten off the Sacred Vessel* . . .' Shortly afterwards Galahad receives Communion 'with great devotion', without any mention of further action on Josephus' part except that of 'taking the Lord's Body from the table'—presumably the Grail's own silver table, since it was not, apparently, from the Altar. (p. 283)

23. William of St. Thierry, *The Mirror of Faith*, trans. G. Webb and A. Walker, Mowbray 1959, ch. 15.

24. Walter de la Mare: Introduction to the *Poems of Edward Thomas*.

25. This is the point at which to refer to two distinguished articles on the interpretation of the *Quest* to which I am much indebted. In *La Mystique de la Grace dans la 'Quête del Saint Graal'*, E. Gilson is concerned (almost to the point of anxiety) to establish the exact identification of the Holy Grail as a symbol of the created grace of God mediated to man by the Holy Spirit. Imprecision or vagueness on this point will in his view darken understanding of the whole work, which he interprets according to St. Bernard's teaching on grace and free will, and the doctrine of Love expounded in *De Diligendo Dei* and the *Sermons on the Song of Songs*. In *Les Grands Secrets du Saint Graal dans la Queste du pseudo-Map* in the collection, *Lumière du Graal*, ed. R. Nelli, 1951, M. Lot-Borodine argues persuasively that the Cistercian mystical theology of the *Quest* is very much more broadly-based than Gilson would allow, and proposes William of St. Thierry's doctrine of the divine image—derived from Origen and Gregory of Nyssa, and expounded in the *Letter to the Brethren of Mont-Dieu*—as a no less fruitful source of inquiry than strictly Bernardine spirituality. While being quite unqualified to engage in debate at their level of scholarship, I have been stimulated by both these articles to take Galahad rather than the Grail itself as a starting-point for inquiry into the theology of the Quest, leaning heavily as will be seen on William of St. Thierry as my guide.

26 'Malory and the Grail Legend', article in the *Dublin Review*, 1944. In a note elsewhere, Williams says that Galahad is 'man's capacity for Christ, or for holy things'. Without wishing to question the validity of Charles Williams' views which are derieved from a deep and creative insight into the Matter of Britain culminating in Malory, I feel it necessary to point the contrast with the entirely different approach of the French *Quest* which, as well as being a work of art, is

also a work of practical spirituality. So, to allow the possibility of a man being totally pre-occupied with God, engaged with all his faculties in the search for God as Galahad is, rather than simply having a Galahad side to his nature—i.e. a more or less developed capacity for spiritual things—would seem to be as crucial to the understanding of this Author's message as it is to the mainstream of Christian tradition to which the *Quest* belongs.

27. It is possible that such passages are an indication of the way in which Cistercian opinion accounted for the failure of the Second Crusade, so ardently promoted by St. Bernard. There is an interesting note on this explanation by G. Constable in *Studies in Mediaeval Cistercian History*, Cistercian Publications 1971, entitled 'A Report of a Lost Sermon by St. Bernard on the Failure of the Second Crusade'.

28. The role of Perceval's sister is as delicately and deftly symbolic as anything in the story. It is worth noting that the character assigned to her makes it impossible to sustain the charge of anti-feminism sometimes brought against the *Quest* (e.g. by Pauphilet). The *Quest* is not anti-feminist but anti-romantic. While Guinevere is bluntly dismissed as one 'who had not made a good confession since she was first married', there is also Perceval's aunt, a blameless recluse with much important intelligence to communicate about the Quest; and his sister rides with the companions as a cherished equal, an object of tenderness and admiration.

29. For a full study of the life and work of William of St. Thierry, see J.M. Déchanet: *William of St. Thierry the Man and his Work*, trans. R. Strachan, Cistercian Studies Series 1972. See also the admirable introductions by Déchanet to *The Golden Epistle, A Letter to the Brethren of Mont-Dieu* and to the *Exposition on the Song of Songs*, both Cistercian Publications 1970. In the following pages where I have quoted severally from William's treatises *On the Nature and Dignity of Love, The Mirror or Faith*, and *The Golden Epistle*, it has been in the tolerable certainty that these works were known to the Author of the *Quest*, even if he understood them to have been written by St. Bernard.

30. Translated by E.S. Pine-Coffin, Penguin Classics edition, 196.

31. This was written 1119-1122, when William was still a Black Benedictine and Abbot of St. Thierry. In the twelfth and thirteenth centuries it was associated with St. Bernard's treatise *On the Love of God* and would be known to this Author as *Liber beati Bernardi de Amore*, see Déchanet op. cit. p. 11.

32. The use of the word *natural* here should not, of course, be confused with its use in the Authorised Version to render I Cor. 2:14 ('the natural man receiveth not the things of God'). The word used by St. Paul is *psuchikos*, in the Vulgate translation *animalis*, and its nearest meaning in English is *animal* or *soulish*.

William's use of *naturalis* (Greek *phusikos* and English *natural*) is perhaps least ambiguously rendered in modern English as *normal*. An old-fashioned but satisfying alternative would be *kindly*, i.e. pertaining or proper to one's own kind. The following lines from Chaucer's *Hous of Fame*, like the passage from the *Confessions*, illustrate the assumption universal in the Middle Ages that all things have their natural or appropriate point of rest:

> Every kindly thing that is
> Hath a kindly stede ther he
> May best in hit conserved be;
> Unto which place every thing
> Through his kindly enclyning
> Moveth for to com to.
> (Book II, 11730 f.)

33. *The Mirror of Faith*, written 1140-1144, is among those of his works which William recommended to the Carthusians of Mont-Dieu for whom he wrote the *Golden Epistle*. (See ch. 25, note 22.)

34. C.S. Lewis in his *Allegory of Love* quotes this from the *De Arte Honeste Amandi* by Andreas Capellanus, an early thirteenth century manual on the laws of Romantic Love. In view of the *Quest*'s fondness for the image of the Fountain associated with the Holy Ghost, Grace, and the Grail, its use in connection with the ethos the *Quest* is bent on exposing is significant.

35. Any attempt to condense into one or even several footnotes the doctrine of the divine image in man which William inherited from St. Augustine and so skilfully grafted into the spiritual anthropology of both Origen and Gregory of Nyssa, would be absurdly inadequate. The reader should consult William's own writings and the work of Dom Déchanet (see note 29). Also, in the chapter on William's teaching in Bouyer, *The Cistercian Heritage*, there is a most useful analytical table of the particular elements of Greek and Latin patristic thought which it was William's great achievement to weld into the living theology which he expounded in his life and writings.

36. *Mirror of Faith*, ch. 2, p. 16.

37. *On the Nature and Dignity of Love*, trans. G. Webb and A. Walker, Mowbrays 1956.

38. *Mirror of Faith*, ch. 3, p. 19.

39. Ibid., ch. 8, p. 30.

40, Ibid., ch. 2, p. 18.

41. Ibid., ch. 11, p. 44.

42. Ibid., ch. 13, p. 41.

43. i.e. in the *Golden Epistle*, written 1144, which within a few years began to be ascribed to St. Bernard. It is uncertain whether the Author of the *Quest* would know it as William's or Bernard's work, but he could not fail to have known a book which gained an immediate and lasting popularity. William's *Exposition of the Song of Songs*, c. 1135, which includes much of the same doctrine, had almost certainly by the early thirteenth century fallen into neglect.

44. *Mirror of Faith*, ch. 1, p. 16.

45. Ibid., ch. 24, p. 67.

46. *Golden Epistle*, II, 15, p. 94.

47. *Mirror of Faith*, ch. 22, p. 64.

48. *Golden Epistle*, I, 17, p. 96.

49. See Dom A. Wilmart: *Auteurs Spirituels et Textes Dévots du Moyen Age Latin* (Paris 1931) for a fascinating note on the Sequence which was first ascribed to the Archbishop of Canterbury by an English Cistercian.

50. 'God is a fire which warms and kindles our hearts. If we feel in our hearts the cold which comes from the devil—for the devil is cold—let us pray to the Lord and He will come and warm our hearts with love for Him and for our neighbour. And before the warmth of His Face the cold of the enemy will be put to flight.' Quoted by V. Lossky in *The Mystical Theology of the Eastern Church*, p. 225. Cf. *Quest, passim*, and especially pp. 132, 91, 173.

51. *Mirror of Faith*, ch. 20, p. 62.

52. Cf. note 22.

53. Cf. Dom Déchanet, op. cit., p. 76: 'William of St. Thierry envisages the Trinity above all as a spring of water welling up to eternal life; as a reality to be contemplated not reasoned about'. Cf. also note 34.

54. By J. Frappier in Loomis, op. cit., note 12. See also Introduction to the Penguin edition of *Quest*, p. 26.

BERNARD AND ABELARD

Love knocks and enters; knowledge stands without.
Hugh of St. Victor

Sister Edmée, SLG

INTRODUCTION

In the centuries following his condemnation at the Council of Sens in 1140 Abelard, although never lacking supporters among specialists, has usually been portrayed at the popular level as an arrogant if clever thinker who over-played a dangerous hand and was deservedly crushed, not a minute before time, by that champion of the true faith St. Bernard. But the rationalism and romanticism of the nineteenth century combined to alter the perspective, since when Abelard has been attracting increasing attention, both scholarly and romantic, and as, in consequence, his stock goes up so St. Bernard's goes down until in most modern studies Bernard is presented (if more implicitly than explicitly) as the villain of the piece whose reactionary zeal cut down a veritable Socrates—'another opponent of self-deception and loose thinking who had been misrepresented as a corrupting influence on the minds of the young'.[1]

Since Abelard's star is still waxing it would be premature to attempt to suggest, as is commonly done when opposing views are set forth, that the truth lies midway between them, even if such seemed to be the case which, to the present writer at least, it does not. There is, indeed, much truth in both extremes. But whether the balance falls in favour of Bernard or Abelard depends less, perhaps, on any objective assessment which, once made, would be available to all, but on individual capacity to apprehend the truths of doctrine. If the truths promulgated by the Church on the basis of Scripture and experience pierce to the marrow of one's being then Bernard's excitement can be shared. If they do not, but are merely intellectually conceded, which would appear by and large to be the situation nowadays among writers on the subject, then sympathy swings to Abelard, and Bernard's invective seems incomprehensible if not repellent.

It is in any case undeniable that to anyone with a contemporary temper of mind Bernard emerges from the conflict with Abelard in an unappealing light, examine the facts as one may. Moreover, even some of Bernard's contemporaries, less sentimental and with a sharper sense of the horror of heresy than ourselves, viewed his handling of the matter with disquiet. For instance, the gentle Abbot of Cluny, Peter the Venerable, unwavering admirer of Bernard as he was, rebuked him severely on this occasion and, welcoming the broken Abelard into his own monastery, insisted on him taking senior rank in the Community, absolved him on his deathbed, and sent a profoundly moving account of his last days to Heloise, thus fulfilling in every detail the role which the world easily recognizes as that of the ideal Christian.

And yet, if Bernard's behaviour towards Abelard 'lacked his usual serenity', as one biographer mildly remarks,[2] it may, nevertheless, no more become us to criticise than for a party at the bottom of a mountain to mark a lack of detachment in a man at the top whose energetic gesticulations are attempting to convey that he can see a fatal danger ahead of them which they cannot. For, however much we may appreciate Abelard's role as questioner and underminer of the *status quo*, in relation to Bernard he was a climber among the foothills the effect of whose excursions into higher altitudes of thought on his followers was, in the long run, more deadly than bracing, as Bernard was able, with such clarity and urgent sense of alarm, to see they would prove to be.

As for Bernard in relation to Abelard, it has become customary to call him a traditionalist. But even if one allows the appellation it is a misleading one to us in the twentieth century, giving rise to semi-conscious associations of a denigratory kind which do little justice to the power and originality of Bernard's genius. It would be more accurate, if less brief, to say that he trod the straight and narrow way of which Christ himself said, '. . . few there be that find it'.

* * * * *

PART I

And the children struggled together within her ... And the Lord said unto her, Two nations are in thy womb, and two manner of people shall be separated from thy bowels; and the one people shall be stronger than the other people; and the elder shall serve the younger.

(The birth of Esau and Jacob. Genesis 25:22-23)

1050-1150. THE EMERGENCE OF MODERN MAN

Current scholarship is disinclined to give credence to the once-held view that Christendom expected dissolution as it approached the year 999 and surged forward with relief into the year 1001,[3] although R.W. Southern, in his essay 'Medieval Humanism' indicates just such a view when he notes a result of it and concludes: 'Then quite suddenly the terror faded and the sun shone.'[4] Certainly much of the evidence continues to be susceptible of the 'day of judgement' interpretation—neither need we laugh. 'Are we prepared to meet our doom?' asked the *Sunday Times* in a leading article (24 November 1974) typical of the prevailing mood, while the religious community in Germany which is refusing postulants in expectation of the imminent end of the world and circulated a news-sheet not long ago headed 'Countdown to disaster', its contents including a full catalogue of prophecies, belongs to twentieth not tenth century history. This latter example may seem too freakish for notice but future historians will doubtless hold it up to the light as symptomatic of *our* expectations of dissolution, gathering gloomily as the century declines.

The difference between then and now is the difference of direction from which the day of judgement is expected. Then it was expected from God. Now it is expected from man. And this change is the logical consequence of that change in the eleventh century when man stopped riveting his attention on God, as a man in the dock for murder might rivet his attention on the judge as he prepares to pronounce sentence, and return it to his natural centre of attention, himself, when a reprieve has been granted. Southern, in the essay referred to above, describes how it was before 1050:

> In the main tradition of the early Middle Ages nearly all the order and dignity in the world was closely associated with supernatural power. There was order in symbolism and ritual, and order in worship and

sacrament, and both of them were elaborate and impressive. Man's links with the supernatural gave his life a framework of order and dignity; but in the natural order the chaos was almost complete. Almost nothing was known about secondary causes in natural events. Rational procedures in law, in government, in medicine, in argument, were scarcely understood or practised even in the most elementary way. Man chiefly knew himself as a vehicle for divine activity. There was a profound sense of the littleness and sinfulness of man. Both physically and mentally human life had narrow limits: only in prayer and penance, in clinging to the saints, was there any enlargement. Man was an abject being, except when he was clad in symbolic garments, performing symbolic and sacramental acts, and holding in his hands the earthly remains of those who already belonged to the spiritual world.

... Perhaps this awe-struck, sacramental view of man's place and powerlessness in the world gives a more satisfactory account of man's situation in the universe than the optimism of the succeeding centuries; and optimism never overcame the final impotence of man and his need for supernatural aid. But there is a sharp change of emphasis after about 1050.[5]

Southern goes on to say that the first signs of the change were to be seen in the monasteries where it 'took the form of a greater concentration on man and on human experience as a means of knowing God', and that one of its most significant moments occurred in Normandy in 1079:

In this year Anselm at Bec entered into the chamber of his mind, excluded everything but the word 'God' and found that suddenly the word articulated itself into a demonstration of God's existence, which he believed to be both new and true. It was new, and whether or not it was true, it was a triumph of an analytical introspective method. It seemed to show that men could find new truths of the greatest general importance simply by looking within themselves. The idea of finding something new was itself new to a generation which had believed itself to be at the end of the road; and to find the new things so close at hand, and so entirely central, was a revelation of the powers that lay within man's mind.[6]

But the revelation of the powers that lie within man's mind are only wholly safe in the hands of a saint. The same year, 1079, saw the birth of Abelard, intellectually the heir of St. Anselm, but in whom spiritual stature was already to degenerate into psychological type. Then in 1090 Bernard, another heir to Anselm, was born who, says Southern, popularized the method of introspection and made it the property of a school of monastic writers, giving the whole exercise a new direction, while not interested, as Anselm had been, in logic and analysis but only in spiritual growth.[7]

Abelard, on the other hand, was only interested in logic and analysis and not at all in spiritual growth, and so we see that by the beginning of the twelfth century a division of Anselm's patrimony had taken place. What had been unified in him, and had thus begun in a certain state of perfection, as new movements generally do, now divided and began to develop independently and at many levels.

The elder son, so to speak, cultivated and brought under control the external world, whether in learning, as it developed in the Schools, or in the first stirrings of scientific discoveries. Chenu in *Nature, Man and Society in the Twelfth Century* says that 'the rise of technology surpassed quantitatively and qualitatively the still elementary awareness that professional and religious men had of the role technology was to play', and among technological advances he lists: the perfecting of machines to harness waterpower and to produce circular motion; mill wheels; hydraulic wheels, which enabled one horse to do the work that formerly required twenty-five; windmills, first used in Europe in 1105; machines that could store power through a system of weights and geared wheels; new armaments that made the old mounted warrior obsolete; new means of transport and travel, giving men increased freedom; the invention of the draft collar for horses and oxen which transformed rural life; and—neither last nor least—the mechanical clock which, says Chenu, 'began to rationalise time, its regularity measuring out a mechanized civilization ... The new gadget was everywhere and cast a new aura round existence which was governed now not by rhythms natural to human life but by a mechanical time'. He goes on to say:

> In this mechanism-minded world, man moved away from a confused trial-and-error approach, became objective and impersonal in his efforts, and grew aware of the complex structures of realities governed by natural laws. Order was no longer merely the scheme proposed by aesthetic imagination or religious conviction; it was experimentally

ascertained and systematically verified, for nature was seen as penetrable and predictable ... Henceforth, the new *homo artifex*, maker of shapes and forms, distinguished between the animate and the mechanical, rid himself of the childish fancies of animism and of the habit of seeing divinity in the marvels of nature. The sacred realm which he secularized by this process no longer possessed any properly religious value for him. He knew its place in the universe better than that.[8]

Of course, man did not 'rid himself of the childish fancies of animism' overnight, nor did he accomplish the secularization of the sacred realm of nature in a year or two. The whole business of coming to 'know better' has, in fact, taken him from then until now—with what results the ecologists of the world, dressed as it were, in sackcloth and ashes, are now repenting. 'Thou turnest man to destruction', says the Psalmist in a mysterious phrase, and goes on: 'Again thou sayest, Come again, ye children of men. For a thousand years in thy sight are but as yesterday.' (Ps. 90:3-4.)

At the intellectual level the cultivation and bringing under control of the external world expressed itself in a sudden passion for learning. Whereas in 1050 education had been hardly come by, if at all, by the beginning of the 1100s there were schools everywhere. There had, indeed, been provision made for them, laid down in various documents from the time of Charlemagne in the eighth century, and although the facilities for education thus provided in theory were not normally available in practice, the consciousness that they ought to be, kept enough of a spark alive in cathedrals and parishes to enable the fire to spread rapidly when it did get going. Guibert of Nogent, who was born in 1053, tells us in his autobiography of the difficulty of finding teachers in his childhood, but by the time Abelard was born in 1079, and Bernard eleven years later, learning had not only spread to every spot where there were students to imbibe it but was of a standard beyond anything that could have been foreseen from the intellectual barrenness of the preceding centuries. Learning had, of course, been available in the monasteries—at the price of becoming a monk—but the educated lay person was, in both senses, exceptional. By 1070 the situation was already noticeably different and thereafter accelerated so that boys of the upper classes who, like Abelard and Bernard, showed signs of intellectual capacity, were sent off to one of the new schools to get a thorough grounding in grammar, rhetoric, dialectic, and the Latin authors instead of being confined to the customary pursuits of fighting and hunting. 'Nothing indeed', says Knowles, 'is a more impressive testimony to the widespread literary culture of the early twelfth century than the emergence of a Bernard from a small provincial school.'[9]

But if Bernard was, providentially, able to take advantage of the facilities provided by the new age, Abelard actually represented it. Bernard was intended by his parents for the Church and thus his learning, first by them and later by himself, was never regarded as more than a means to an end. In Abelard's case the emphasis was always on learning for its own sake, as the opening paragraphs of his autobiography show:

> My father had acquired some knowledge of letters before he was a soldier, and later on his passion for learning was such that he intended all his sons to have instruction in letters before they were trained to arms. His purpose was fulfilled. I was his firstborn, and being specially dear to him had the greatest care taken over my education. For my part, the more rapid and easy my progress in my studies, the more eagerly I applied myself, until I was so carried away by my love of learning that I renounced the glory of a soldier's life, made over my inheritance and rights of the eldest son to my brothers, and withdrew from the court of Mars in order to kneel at the feet of Minerva. I preferred the weapons of dialectic to all the other teachings of philosophy, and armed with these I chose the conflicts of disputation instead of the trophies of war. I began to travel about in several provinces disputing, like a true peripatetic philosopher, wherever I had heard there was keen interest in the art of dialectic.[10]

Peripatetic, meaning 'one who walks about', was the name given to the followers of Aristotle from the circumstance that he taught in the portico (*peripatos* = 'for walking about') of the Lyceum at Athens. A meaningful etymology for, as Abelard shows, the peripatetic philosophers of the twelfth century did indeed walk about, 'seeking whom they might devour' in debate. Their method was based on a structure of question (*quaestio*), argument (*disputatio*), and conclusion (*sententia*), namely, posing, discussing, and resolving problems by means of question and answer, and was quite new when Abelard adopted it. The traditional manner of teaching had been to expound passages of Scripture by means of appropriate glosses and commentaries—imposed, no doubt, upon them. One visualizes a somewhat ponderous master, lecturing to silent, respectful, and unquestioning students. It is not surprising, then, that the entry of the peripatetic philosopher, 'more subtle than any beast of the field'—not to mention any master in the schools, according to Abelard's account—enlivened learning with his stimulatingly conversational approach: 'Did God say . . . ?'

* * * * *

In the cathedral of St. Lazarus at Autun, just a few miles from Clairvaux, and contemporaneously with ten years of Bernard's abbacy, the genius of Gislebertus was at work (c. 1125-1135) carving out in stone a pictorial representation of the beliefs and ideas of his times. 'There is little doubt', say Grivot and Zarnecki in their book on him, 'that Gislebertus wished to convey a moral message in his sculpture; in fact, he was closer in spirit to St. Bernard than any other sculptor of the twelfth century.'[11] And yet, close in space and spirit though he may have been, his figure of Eve sums up with a wonderful sympathy and fascination, and with not the slightest hint of a moral message, the delight men were experiencing in tasting afresh of the tree of knowledge. Reclining in a horizontal position, suggestive of the new age as against the old which had been vertically orientated, or perhaps because Eve always symbolises the horizontal, she is calling men from behind a cupped hand to the feast of reason, her own eyes already wide open as the serpent had promised:

For God doth know that in the day ye eat thereof, then your eyes shall be opened, and ye shall be as gods, knowing good and evil. (Gen. 3:5.)

All around her in the cathedral are figures who have achieved their destiny: the contemplative tranquillity of the blessed side by side with the terrifying monstrosity of the damned, each on their way to the eternal habitations of heaven or hell. But Eve is still in the process of achieving; no judgement has yet been passed on her. Meanwhile, as Scripture calls her, and as Gislebertus so marvellously conveys, she is 'the mother of all the living'.

There was, however, at that time an actual, not a figurative mother who, at one of those crucial moments of choice which affect the whole course of a life, influenced her son against the call of Eve, thus providing the Church with the greatest counterpoint figure of the age.

ST. BERNARD AND THE SCHOOLS

Everyone said that he was a youth with great prospects, and if externals were anything to judge by, he must have been; for his body was well proportioned, his face pleasing, his manner gentle and courteous, his mind keen, and his speech persuasive and appealing. Many careers in the world lay open to him, and success seemed assured in whatever he would decide to do.

William of St. Thierry, *Life of St. Bernard*[12]

Success hardly seemed assured, however, when he decided to enter the monastery at Cîteaux, a small, struggling community, founded only fifteen years earlier and already showing signs of closing down through want of vocations, lack of perseverance among many of the founding brethren, and a number of deaths due to unhealthy conditions and undernourishment.

Bernard's family had no objection to his becoming a monk. But they had every objection to him becoming a monk at Cîteaux instead of in one of the comfortable Cluniac houses in the neighbourhood where they could have kept up contact and, no doubt, catered for those little extras which even the best establishments are liable to lack. Bernard himself later wrote: 'I chose Cîteaux in preference to Cluny not because I was not aware that the life was excellent and lawful but because "I am a thing of flesh and blood, sold unto the slavery of sin." I was conscious that my weak character needed a strong medicine.'[13]

But decisions which have to last a whole life must be made by the whole man and it seems that at first Bernard's decision to become a Cistercian, based as it was on reason and self-knowledge of the highest order, did not yet encompass his entire being. The cord which kept him bound was precisely that desire for learning which was affecting the men of his world with such force, and because of it his family were able to persuade him to go to Germany for further studies before committing himself to Cîteaux. The extent to which this plan was in accord with Bernard's literary ambitions is revealed by the violence with which he subsequently reacted against those ambitions. But while still pursuing them William of St. Thierry tells us that the memory of his holy mother, Aleth, who had died in 1104 when Bernard was fourteen, began to fill his mind 'so that he seemed to see her coming to him, reproaching and upbraiding him that she had not brought him up with such love and care so that he could adopt this empty kind of existence, and that it was not for the fulfilment of such worldly ambitions that she had brought him into the world'.[14]

The crucial moment of choice came when, during the first stage of his journey, he was so disquieted by these thoughts that he stopped and, entering a church, gave himself to prayer. 'If, therefore, thine eye be single thy whole body shall be full of light' (Matt. 6:22), and from thenceforth Bernard was possessed of the single eye of the true monk, emerging not only full of light but, as William of St. Thierry says, 'like the flame which turns the forest into a roaring blaze and then goes on to burn the mountains black'[15]—the first victims of the blaze being the twenty-nine relations and friends whom he led on to Cîteaux within a few months.

The recruitment of this company, which included four out of five of Bernard's brothers (the fifth being too young—the only impediment permitted by Bernard—but inevitably joining him as soon as he was old enough), and their arrival at the monastery, where one pictures an abbot interrupted in his melancholy task of winding up the place with the news that thirty young men were without desiring admittance to the life,[16] makes for a story of fairy-tale timelessness. In fact, when seen against the rise of the schools, it takes on a meaning which suggests an absolute if invisible dependence of one situation upon the other. For, as it is said that wherever stinging nettles grow there also will be found a healing dock leaf, so this company of young men can be seen as forming the spearhead of a movement from which the antidote to what was pernicious in the passion for learning might be applied to society. Or, as the monks themselves understood the matter, 'whose presence, acting like leaven, worked through the whole lump and kept it from corruption'.[17]

Three years after his entry into Cîteaux Bernard was sent by his abbot, Stephen Harding, to establish Clairvaux, and this foundation in turn produced sixty-five daughter houses before the end of Bernard's life, while Cîteaux itself continued to found houses at an incredible rate. It was 'schools against schools', as Gilson says in a passage the whole of which is an admirable summary of the thought of the time:

> No one, even in the twelfth century, entertained any naive illusion about a primitive Church in which all the members were perfect Christians. The number of the saints had always been small. The Gospel, since it was preached to all the world, had never been received save in the measure of the capacity of the recipients; but it was precisely on

that account that even from the earliest days there was formed a small inner group of perfect imitators of Christ, whose presence, acting like a leaven, worked through the whole lump and kept it from corruption. Immediately after the death of Christ the Apostles themselves would seem to have formed a group of this kind, that is to say a school of masters whose very life was a lesson, who, for the rest, taught nothing save the Gospel offered to all, and whom few nevertheless cared to join precisely on account of the rigorous way in which they put its teachings into practice. 'And they were all with one accord in Solomon's Porch. But of the rest no man durst join himself to them, but the people magnified them.' (Acts 5:12-13.) These then were the first monks, and from their example we learn what from the first had always been the meaning of the monastic life:—that is, the life of an élite who, by preaching and by example, maintain the full spirit of the Gospel in a world unable to bear it.

The name attached to this group by the author of the Cistercian *Exordium* is typically Benedictine: it is a school, the School of the Primitive Church. Already at the outset of his Rule, St. Benedict had proclaimed that he intended to open a school of the service of the Lord. The Cistercians had many good reasons of their own for adopting the expression and investing it with new significance. Twelfth-century France was filled with schools of profane science and ancient letters. There was not only Saint-Vorles, where the young Bernard had pursued his studies with a programme that might well astonish, not to say disquiet, a soul so eager for Christ, there were Paris, Reims, Laon, Chartres—so many other famous names but always the same masters: Cicero, Virgil, Ovid, Horace, eloquent spokesmen of a world that had never read the Gospel. Why not invoke another master, the only master who has the words of eternal life? . . . Cîteaux, Clairvaux and Signy were then to stand over against Reims, Laon, Paris and Chartres, schools against schools, and to vindicate in a Christian land the rights of a teaching more Christian than that with which the minds of guileless youths were wont to be poisoned.[18]

But the most powerful spokesmen of a world that had never read the Gospel were Plato and Aristotle. Cicero and the rest may have formed men's minds and thus to a considerable extent influenced their behaviour, but Plato and Aristotle struck at the roots of men's being. Life looked different, *was* different when studied through those great eyes—and now suddenly it was. 'This change was not occasioned by any discovery of ancient texts', says Knowles. 'The works of Boethius ... had always been available, but whereas in the past they had evoked no response in the minds of their readers, they were now appreciated in all their dynamic force.'[19]

Just how dynamic those forces were may be seen on the one hand in the revival of Aristotelian dialectic which produced the peripatetic philosophers; and on the other hand in the all-pervasiveness of an adapted Platonic mysticism which inspired not only most of the religious literature of the times but issued in the great masterpieces of Gothic architecture, thus realizing in Christendom an aesthetic which held the field in art and music down to the eighteenth century.

The twelfth century, then, saw a new and universal ascendance of the two Greek minds arising solely out of its own psychology and not as a result of the arrival of fresh texts—as was to happen in the next century. Coleridge thought that each of us is from birth either a Platonist or an Aristotelian, and had he been referring to the twelfth century he would perhaps have been right for one has the impression that everybody was at that time a Greek of one kind or another.[20] Everybody, that is, except Bernard—and he was a Hebrew of the Hebrews. For the real division in human types is between Jew and Greek, with the Platonic and Aristotelian psychologies forming a sub-division of the latter. Bernard, alone among the giants of the time, represent the 'Jew' type, which explains why to the Greek cast of mind he sticks out from the century like a sore thumb. But 'salvation is of the Jews' (John 4:22), and it is not too much to say that Bernard was raised up in the providence of God to save the brilliant opening of a new era for the Gospel, and to check the excesses into which man's excitement with new knowledge inevitably leads him.

> You must not think that I am scoffing at knowledge or blaming the learned and forbidding the study of letters! [he said to his monks] Far from it! I know well what service her scholars have rendered and are rendering to the Church, both by refuting her enemies and by instructing the simple. But it is written that 'knowledge puffeth up,' while in another place, 'He that addeth knowledge addeth also grief.' There is a difference, you see, between these two: one knowledge fills a man with pride, the other saddens him. And obviously the latter is that

which ministers to our salvation, for God heals the broken-hearted but abhors the proud. All knowledge which is founded on the truth is indeed good in itself. But you, who are set on working out your salvation with fear and trembling, and with all speed, because the time is short, must give priority to the studies which most nearly concern it. Doctors tell us—do they not?—that part of the art of medicine consists in knowing what food should be taken, and in what order and manner they are best consumed. For though all foods God has created are good in themselves, you may easily make them far from good *for you* if you do not take them in the proper order and the proper way. And the same applies to the various branches of knowledge.

But I had better send you to the master, for this teaching is not ours but his... 'If any man,' he says, 'thinks that he knows anything, he does not yet know it as he ought to know.' It is the manner of knowing that he singles out as the important thing; and that includes the order of our study, the effort we devote to it, and the end we have in view in undertaking it. As to the order, that must come first which will forward our salvation; as to the effort, the most must be expended on the studies that kindle us to love; and as to the object that we have in view, we must seek to acquire knowledge, not from vainglory or curiosity or anything like that, but only for the sake of our own edification or that of our neighbour. For there are some who desire knowledge merely for its own sake; and that is shameful curiosity. And there are others who desire to know in order that they may themselves be known; and that is vanity, disgraceful too. Others, again, desire knowledge in order to acquire money or preferment by it; that too is a discreditable quest. But there are also some who desire knowledge that they may build up others' souls with it; and that is charity. Others again, desire it that they themselves may be built up thereby; and that is prudence.

Out of all these types, the last two only put knowledge to right use. All the others merely illustrate the truth of the Apostle's saying that 'knowledge puffeth up.'[21]

PETER ABELARD

At last I came to Paris, where dialectic had long been particularly flourishing, and joined William of Champeaux who at the time was the supreme master of the subject, both in reputation and in fact. I stayed in his school for a time, but though he welcomed me at first he soon took a violent dislike to me because I set out to refute some of his arguments and frequently reasoned against him. On several occasions I proved myself his superior in debate . . . This was the beginning of the misfortunes which have dogged me to this day, and as my reputation grew, so other men's jealousy was aroused. (*H. C.*, p. 58.)

Thus the third paragraph of Abelard's 'Letter of consolation to his friend', traditionally entitled *Historia Calamitatum*. He goes on to describe how he subsequently forced William to abandon his position on the question of 'universals', and hounds him, through several pages, into a monastery where, licking his wounds and gnashing his teeth with envy, he remained, having lost hope of future worldly fame in the face of Abelard's greater brilliance. Other contemporary accounts reveal William as a saintly character. No doubt Abelard contributed greatly to his sanctification.

The next subject of attack is the famous Master Anselm of Laon who, according to Abelard, became equally consumed with jealousy, even losing his head and forbidding Abelard to continue his work of interpretation in the place where he [Anselm] taught—'an act of sheer spite and calumny such as had never been directed at anyone before'.[22] Abelard then settled in Paris and taught for several years in the school of Notre Dame:

. . . As soon as I began my course of teaching I set myself to complete the commentaries on Ezekiel which I had started at Laon. These proved so popular with their readers that they judged my reputation to stand as high for my interpretation of Scripture as it had previously done for philosophy. The numbers in the school increased enormously as the students gathered there eager for instruction in both subjects, and the wealth and fame this brought me must be well known to you.
(*H. C.*, p. 65.)

All this provides a strong contrast to Bernard's view that the acquisition of knowledge is only rightly undertaken in the causes of charity and prudence—two qualities conspicuously lacking in Abelard. Neither is he better endowed with the two kinds of knowledge required by Bernard: self-knowledge, leading to the knowledge of God. For the *Historia Calamitatum* exemplifies the fact that self-revelation is not only not the same as self-knowledge but may even be inimical to it, although candour certainly coincides with truth in his next paragraph:

> ... Success always puffs up fools with pride, and worldly security weakens the spirit's resolution and easily destroys it through carnal temptations. I began to think myself the only philosopher in the world, with nothing to fear from anyone, and so I yielded to the lusts of the flesh.

* * * *

PART II

By thy great wisdom and by thy traffick hast thou increased thy riches, and thine heart is lifted up because of thy riches. Therefore, thus saith the Lord God: Because thou hast set thine heart as the heart of God, behold, therefore I will bring strangers upon thee, the terrible of the nations; and they shall draw their swords against the beauty of thy wisdom, and they shall defile thy brightness.   Ezekiel 28:5-7

Writers on Abelard have remained mostly silent in face of the appalling personal disaster of his mutilation, some indeed so silent that in otherwise full accounts of him they have not even mentioned it. But usually it is treated as a separate theme: Abelard the thinker on the one hand; Abelard the lover on the other. In either case it is seen as an isolated event, the consequent of an interruption of passion into his otherwise exclusively cerebral career, terrible to contemplate, yet unrelated to the significance of his life as a whole.

In this section I shall, on the contrary, suggest that the castration of Abelard is central to his psychology, and that if one places it thus instead of at the periphery, his life takes on a meaning which illuminates man's case when he begins to develop independently of his Creator. As we have seen, this independent development began at the turn of the eleventh century and had reached the point of establishing itself by the time Abelard came to represent it. Viewed in this light, Abelard is seen to stand at the dawn of our millenium as a symbol of man's ultimate impotence. He thus takes on a character of biblical dimensions, another Esau who, having renounced his birthright, is left to live by the sword (Gen. 27:40), that is, the two-edged sword of truth which cuts both ways and of which, when wielded on its own merits and in its own strength, our Lord said: 'They that take the sword shall perish with the sword'. (Matt. 26:52.)

My thesis, then, is that the cause of Abelard's castration lay not in his liaison with Heloise but in the attitude of mind exemplified by the following passage:

> One day it happened that after a session of *Sentences* we students were joking amongst ourselves, when someone rounded on me and asked what I thought of the reading of the Holy Scriptures, when I had hitherto studied only philosophy. I replied that concentration on such reading was most beneficial for the salvation of the soul, but that I found it most surprising that for educated men the writings or glosses of the Fathers themselves were not sufficient for interpreting their commentaries without further instruction. There was general laughter, and I was asked by many of those present if I could or would tackle this myself. I said I was ready to try if they wished. Still laughing, they shouted 'Right, that's settled! Take some commentary on a little-known text and we'll test what you say.' Then they all agreed on an extremely obscure prophecy of Ezekiel. I took the commentary and promptly invited them all to hear my interpretation the very next day. They then pressed unwanted advice on me, telling me not to hurry over something so important but to remember my inexperience and give longer thought to working out and confirming my exposition. I replied indignantly that it was not my custom to benefit by practice, but I relied on my own intelligence, and either they must come to my lecture at the time of my choosing or I should abandon it altogether.
>
> At my first lecture there were certainly not many people present, for everyone thought it absurd that I could attempt this so soon, when up to now I had made no study at all of the Scriptures. But all those who came approved, so that they commended the lecture warmly, and urged me to comment on the text on the same lines as my lecture. The news brought people who had missed my first lecture flocking to the second

and third ones, all alike most eager to make copies of the glosses which I had begun with on the first day. (*H. C.*, pp. 64f.)

Clearly Abelard had found in dialectic a useful and legitimate key but, as one writer describes it, dialectic 'had the same corrosive effect upon true religion and sound learning that psychology has in our day. It was essentially a study of form rather than of content, and so it was a playground of critical minds, concerned with every aspect of intellectual inquiry while sitting lightly to the subject-matter of any of them.'[1]

Against the success of such an approach to the Scriptures, the Cistercians were to develop the monastic tradition of *lectio divina*, making the prayerful pondering of the Bible the centre of their lives; and in order to support the suggestion of a connection between Abelard's attitude to the exposition of Scripture and his castration, it is necessary to discuss that tradition for the thesis depends on the view of the Bible embodied in it.

The attitude of the monk, then, to *lectio divina* is that of a man who has come to himself and knows at last that he is in a far country. He knows, that is, that he is a sinner, alienated from God and habituated to the pig-sty of his own sins. But now he *remembers* and, in reading the Scriptures, he rises and begins the long return. Every word draws him nearer because every word is the Word of his Father to whom he will say, when he gets near enough, 'Father, I have sinned against heaven, and in thy sight, and am no more worthy to be called thy son' (Luke 15:21). But one of the difficulties of the way back is that the language in which the Father speaks has been forgotten. And so the monk, in reading the Word of God, *listens* as though to a foreign tongue in which he is a beginner. He is anxious to get it right as the servant of a great king is anxious to interpret his lord's commands correctly, or as the lover is anxious to understand the desires of the beloved. But, alas, the king talks in riddles and the beloved whispers inaudibly—or so it seems to the monk, for he is still in the land of unlikeness. Sometimes, perhaps even often, the Word reveals its meaning to him and then he is filled with a peculiar joy. But it is a joy always tempered by penitence for he knows that in respect of the Word he has squandered his inheritance and lost his rights and that everything he gains henceforth is pure gift. In any case, his primary purpose in pondering the Scriptures is not for the sake of enlightenment—which might do no more for him than keep him comfortable among the pigs—but for conversion of life. And so St. Benedict writes at the beginning of his *Rule*:

> Up with us then at last, for the Scripture arouseth us, saying: *Now is the hour for us to rise from sleep.* Let us open our eyes to the divine light, and let us hear with attentive ears the warning that the divine voice crieth daily to us: *Today if ye will hear his voice, harden not your hearts* . . . For the Apostle saith: *Knowest thou not that the patience of God inviteth to repentance?* While the merciful Lord saith: *I will not the death of a sinner, but that he be converted and live.*[2]

Such is the disposition of the monk towards the Scriptures, and the results of it are crucial. For not only is it that he listens attentively to the Word as to a strange, half-understood, half-heard, longed-for language, but that in so doing he *receives* the Word into his soul as seed into the womb or, as in the parable of the sower, into that good ground which brings forth fruit with patience, some an hundredfold, some sixty and some thirty. (Matt. 13:23.) And the seed is Christ who is thus forever being conceived and growing in the heart until, transformed by his indwelling presence, the monk can say with St. Paul: 'I live, yet not I, but Christ liveth in me' (Gal. 2:20).[3]

Now if the monk represents man in fruitful union with the Word of God, Abelard, I suggest, represents man in a barren relationship to it. Barren because he was unable to surrender himself to it and so permit it to penetrate into the silent depths of his being where it could have taken root and grown *within* him. For the principal characteristic we need to note about Abelard is that although he was immensely pious—sometimes movingly so—religion for him remained external. He embodied, as we have seen, that new drive to bring the external world under control, and if control is the aim the subject of it must be kept under control and not allowed to take it. Hence his unceasingly discursive temperament, incapable of pausing to question itself, resisted every exercise by which Christ might have entered and been quickened in his soul. Consequently his theology reflected this failure and, in turn, his life reflected and was ruined by his theology. For Christ saves from within, and except he be within no amount of Christ without can save us. So, when Bernard came to write his 'Treatise against Abelard' he seized vigorously on this weakness: 'Did Jesus, then, teach righteousness and not *bestow* it? Did he show charity and not *infuse* it, and did he so return to his heaven?'[4]

What profits it [Bernard goes on] that Jesus should instruct us if he did not first restore us by his grace? Or are we in vain instructed if the body of sin is not first destroyed in us, that we should no more serve sin? If all the benefit that we derive from Christ consists in the exhibition of his virtues, it follows that Adam must be said to harm us only by the exhibition of sin. But in truth the medicine given was proportioned to the disease. *For as in Adam all die, even so in Christ shall all be made alive.* As is the one so is the other. If the life which Christ gives is nothing else but his instruction, the death which Adam gave is in like manner only his instruction; so that the one by his example leads men to sin, the other by his example and his word leads them to a holy life and to love him. But if we ... confess that by generation and not by example was the sin of Adam imparted to us, and by sin death, let us confess that it is necessary for righteousness to be restored to us by Christ, not by instruction *but by regeneration* ... And if this be so, how can Peter [Abelard] say that the only purpose and cause of the Incarnation was that he might enlighten the world by the light of his wisdom and inflame it with love of him? Where, then, is redemption? There come from Christ, he says, merely illumination and enkindling to love. Whence come redemption and liberation?[5]

Whence, for Abelard, indeed, since, as Bernard rightly shows in this passage, he believed only in an external Christ—with what results in his life let us briefly examine.

THE LOVER

Abelard was about thirty-eight when, having been hitherto, as he tells us, entirely continent, the energy which had animated his intellect until then now began to slip and to animate him, as it were, whence it had arisen. To meet this new situation he resolved to take a mistress and, circumstances providentially placing in his care the young Heloise, he decided to bring her to his bed, confident that he should have easy success. 'For', he goes on, 'at that time I had youth and exceptional good looks as well as my great reputation to recommend me, and I feared no rebuff from any woman I might choose to honour with my love.' (*H.C.*, p. 66.)

This is a brave style for a man whose single essay into the lists of love was to unseat and enslave him so humiliatingly for, far from being in control of the situation the situation immediately took control of him and his infatuation became obsessive, with disastrous consequences on his career:

> It became utterly boring for me to have to go to the school, and equally wearisome to remain there and to spend my days on study when my nights were sleepless with love-making. As my interest and concentration flagged, my lectures lacked all inspiration and were merely repetitive; I could do no more than repeat what had been said long ago, and when inspiration did come to me, it was for writing love-songs, not the secrets of philosophy. (*H. C.*, p. 68.)

For a man whose primary passion lay in learning, and the life which went with it, he found himself in a fearful impasse. The more he must have desired to be free from the secondary passion for Heloise the more helplessly enmeshed he became.

And so began a series of futile efforts to free himself, which can be seen as the inevitable consequence of his belief in goodness as example and not as indwelling. In other words, his weapons in the struggle were all external to him and when they failed—as one by one they did—he could turn to nothing within, since he knew of nothing within, and was unable to hope that the victory of him who 'was in all points tempted like as we are, yet without sin' (Heb. 4:15) could save him. And, lacking that hope, liberation, for him, lay only in that which actually occurred.

His first major step in the struggle to free himself from what he later described as the 'depths of shame to which my unbridled lust had consigned our bodies, until no reverence for decency or for God, even during the days of Our Lord's Passion, or of the greater sacraments, could keep me from wallowing in this mire',[6] was to resolve upon marrying Heloise. He evidently hoped, by being united to Heloise in the sacred relationship of marriage, to cool the ardour which a clandestine situation inevitably fans. But as the morality of the times preferred celibacy in its teachers, he would have lost face had the marriage been known and so he insisted on it being kept secret, thus losing the benefit of freedom from 'unbridled lust' which can reasonably be expected as the reward of undertaking the marriage bond.

Heloise understood at once the implications of this decision and resisted it with all possible force. With unblinking vanity Abelard repeats the arguments she brought against it (those which appealed to him, that is. She apparently had others (L. I., p. 114) about which, after reading the *Historia*, she accused him of keeping silent):

What honour could she win, she protested, from a marriage which would dishonour me and humiliate us both? The world would justly exact punishment from her if she removed such a light from its midst. Think of the curses, the loss to the Church and grief of philosophers which would greet such a marriage! Nature had created me for all mankind—it would be a sorry scandal if I should bind myself to a single woman and submit to such base servitude. She absolutely rejected this marriage, it would be nothing but a disgrace and a burden to me. Along with the loss of my reputation she put before me the difficulties of marriage . . .

which Abelard himself puts before the reader for the next three and a half pages concluding with:

But at last she saw that her attempts to dissuade me were making no impression on my foolish obstinacy, and she could not bear to offend me; so amidst deep sighs and tears she ended in these words: 'We shall both be destroyed. All that is left us is suffering as great as our love has been.' In this, as the whole world knows, she showed herself a true prophet. (*H.C.*, p. 74.)

Indeed, for then their troubles really began—to the pained surprise of the propounder of the ethic of pure intention.

Their meetings became increasingly few and furtive. Before the marriage Abelard had not been afraid to have a mistress but now he was fearful of it being known that he had a wife. So Fulbert, Heloise's guardian (allegedly her uncle but fulfilling a role in the drama which suggests—beyond doubt in my view—that he was in fact her father), began to spread the news of the secret marriage and was enraged when Heloise denied it. At this point Abelard removed her to the convent at Argenteuil where she had been brought up and, quite inexplicably on the face of it, had her dressed in the religious habit. What was his motive?

As far as I am aware no attention has been paid to this significant fact, and yet it seems worth noticing. For here, in this unremarked detail, we find confirmation in his actions of the defects in his thought. By placing Heloise in a consecrated place and dressing her in the externals of a consecrated life he evidently intended to render her—who was his wife—untouchable, the obverse of that error of which St. Paul speaks: 'He that eateth and drinketh unworthily eateth and drinketh damnation to himself, not discerning the Lord's body' (I Cor. 11:29). That is to say, he who puts his trust in the externals of religion, failing to discern and so to correspond with the inner reality, will be damned by those very things he hopes will save him.

And so it was. Fulbert, whose perceptions had apparently been sharpened by suffering, interpreted this action as Abelard's easy way of ridding himself of Heloise by making her a nun (*H. C.*, p. 75), and prepared his revenge. Meanwhile Heloise meditated on the Bible in her convent and Abelard expounded it in his school. His efforts at self-liberation seemed to be working. The *mise en scène* was complete. The axe, so to speak, was ready to fall.

And for Abelard it finally fell on the occasion he visited Heloise:

> You know what my uncontrollable desire did with you there, actually in a corner of the refectory, since we had nowhere else to go. I repeat, you know how shamelessly we behaved on that occasion in so hallowed a place, dedicated to the most holy Virgin. Even if our other shameful behaviour was ended, this alone would deserve far heavier punishment . . . (L.4, p. 146.)

* * * * *

'Be careful of what you want for you shall surely have it'—warns an Arab proverb. Abelard had been driven step by step through a particular, and particularly compelling, situation to want the final effecting in his body of that which was already a reality in his soul. But the fulfilment of an unrecognized wish inevitably evokes a reaction against it. Abelard's first reaction to the disaster—or, rather, his second, because his first reaction to every disaster always concerned his reputation, his perennial preoccupation—was that the justice of God had struck him in the part of the body with which he had sinned; while chief among many other humiliating reflections he was 'also appalled to remember that according to the cruel letter of the Law, a eunuch is such an abomination to the Lord that men made eunuchs by the amputation or mutilation of their members are forbidden to enter a church . . .' (*H. C.*, p. 76.) But later his satisfaction at being thus permanently delivered from the 'contagion of carnal impurity' (L. 4, p. 148) emerged in the view that he had been uniquely singled out, not for God's justice but for his mercy:

> How mercifully did he want me to suffer so much only in that member, the privation of which would also further the salvation of my soul without defiling my body nor preventing any performance of my duties! ... So when divine grace cleansed rather than deprived me of those vile members which from their practice of utmost indecency are called 'the parts of shame' and have no proper name of their own, what else did it do but remove a foul imperfection in order to preserve purity?
> (L.4, p. 148.)

He then goes on to show that he is superior to Origen because blameless of the deed[7] and more favoured than St. Paul who besought the Lord to rid him of this thorn in the flesh, but was not heard.

> ... In my case, through God's compassion, it was done by another's hand. I do not incur blame, I escape it. I deserve death and gain life. I am called but hold back; I persist in crime and am pardoned against my will. The Apostle prays and is not heard, he persists in prayer and is not answered. Truly the Lord takes thought for me. I will go then and declare how much the Lord has done for my soul. (L.4, p. 149.)

All this, and much else besides, gives an overwhelming impression that Abelard is missing the point. He rightly feels his case to be unique but his moralizings obscure the cause. For in him we can see the truth that the cause of lust becoming uncontrollable in direct opposition to the will is to be found not in itself but in the activity of pride, in particular in that aspect called presumption—Abelard's chief characteristic.

Heloise, on the other hand, although inclined to play Echo to Abelard's Narcissus, does not moralize about their relationship. Jean Leclercq points out that the contrast between them 'appears even in the vocabulary applied to the same experiences: when Heloise speaks of "desires", "delights", "sensuous pleasures" as being realities which were and still are "sweet" and "agreeable", Abelard mentions only "turpitudes", "impurities", "fornications", and "abominations".[8] Heloise does not reflect Abelard's censorious attitude because—she was in love with him—and lust is always subject to love. Consequently it remained in her as an ever-present power, giving energy both to her spiritual development and to her practical abilities. At the same time her constant and agonizing awareness of it kept her humble ('I do not seek a crown of victory; it is sufficient for me to avoid danger ...' (L.3, p. 135)) and free from the illusion of loving God for himself alone—an illusion with which those who enter the religious state of their own free choice are, in the nature of the case, liable to be afflicted.[9]

Abelard, indeed, understood that, in comparison with himself, Heloise had the better part for 'the one who must always strive there is also a crown ... But no crown is waiting for me because no cause of striving remains'. (L.4, p. 154.) While earlier in the same letter he exclaims to the still young but already revered abbess: 'How great an interest the talent of your own wisdom pays daily to the Lord in the many spiritual daughters you have borne for him, while I remain totally barren and labour in vain amongst the sons of perdition!' (L.4, p. 150.)

In spite of which he is clearly thinking primarily of himself when he sums up his feelings about the purpose of his castration: 'See, then, how greatly the Lord was concerned for us, as if he were reserving us for some great ends, and was indignant or grieved because our knowledge of letters, the talents which he had entrusted to us, were not being used to glorify his name ... (L.4, p. 149.)

THE THINKER

Abelard, being now about forty years of age, began at once those writings and lecturings which were to occupy him for the next twenty years of his life until the final disaster at Sens. Having entered the abbey of Saint-Denis he had scarcely, he tells us, recovered from his wound before 'the clerks came thronging round to pester the abbot and myself with repeated demands that I should now for the love of God continue the studies which hitherto I had pursued only in desire for wealth and fame.' And so, he writes:

> ... I first applied myself to lecturing on the basis of our faith by analogy with human reason, and composed a theological treatise 'On the Unity and Trinity of God' for the use of my students who were asking for human and logical reasons on this subject, and demanded something intelligible rather than mere words. In fact they said that words were useless if the intelligence could not follow them, that nothing could be believed unless it was first understood, and that it was absurd for anyone to preach to others what neither he nor those he taught could grasp with the understanding: the Lord himself criticised such 'blind guides of blind men.' After the treatise had been seen and read by many

people it began to please everyone, as it seemed to answer all questions alike on this subject. It was generally agreed that the questions were peculiarly difficult and the importance of the problem was matched by the subtlety of my solution. (*H.C.*, p. 78.)

However, this treatise, which solved according to human and logical reasons, and to the satisfaction of young students, the problems of the Trinity, did not, after all, please everyone and, in 1121, two years after his mutilation, it was condemned at the Council of Soissons.

That this Council was as brutish in its way as Fulbert's revenge had been may be allowed from Abelard's account. The proceedings, indeed, gave him ample opportunity for drawing his favourite comparison—that between himself and Christ. But if the situation bore marks of similarity they were confined to the situation and did not extend to Abelard's own behaviour which signally failed to follow that example he held to be the means of grace. For whereas when Jesus 'was accused of the chief priests and elders, he answered nothing' (Matt. 27:12), Abelard played into his enemies hands by being all too eager to justify himself, pouring forth a torrent of explanations, until silenced, which only succeeded in further confusing the issue and hardening opinion against him.

My former betrayal seemed small in comparison with the wrongs I now had to endure, and I wept much more for the injury done to my reputation than for the damage to my body, for that I had brought upon myself through my own fault, but this open violence had come upon me only because of the purity of my intentions and love of our Faith which had compelled me to write. (*H.C.*, p. 85.)

Happily the damage to his reputation was soon repaired and he was able to escape from the goodness and kindness of the abbot and monks of St. Médard, where he had been confined after the condemnation, back to his own monastery which, being 'completely worldly and depraved' (*H.C.*, p. 77), provided an ambience conducive to his sense of moral superiority—now added to his sense of intellectual superiority.

Needless to say he did not last at Saint-Denis. While reading Bede he discovered that their patron was not to be identified with the Dionysius the Areopagite of Acts 17:34, a discovery he pointed out to some of the brethren 'by way of a joke'. No one laughed, however, and he was compelled to flee from their lack of humour on the subject. In due course—his one piece of fortune in the midst of all his calamities—he was able to take possession of a piece of land in a lonely spot under the jurisdiction of the Bishop of Troyes.

At first he dedicated this place to the Trinity but re-named it, very unusually, the Paraclete on account of the comfort in his despair he had found there. His sensitivity to criticism obliged him to defend this name at length (*H. C.*, pp. 91 f.), and with his usual overtones of self-pity, but it is here we get a glimpse for the first time in the *Historia* of a serious and independent thinker. It is here also, in his life at the Paraclete, that Abelard's attraction for the times is most clearly demonstrated; for it is one thing to flock to a teacher in the town where one already is, quite another to go after him into the country, as Abelard so vividly describes:

> No sooner was this known than the students began to gather there from all parts, hurrying from cities and towns to inhabit the wilderness, leaving large mansions to build themselves little huts, eating wild herbs and coarse bread instead of delicate food, spreading reeds and straw in place of soft beds and using banks of turf for tables. (*H. C.*, pp. 88 f.)

Abelard spent about three years in this place, while his pupils provided 'all I needed, unasked, food, clothing, work on the land as well as building expenses ... As my oratory could not hold even a modest proportion of their numbers, they were obliged to enlarge it, and improved it by building in wood and stone.' Inevitably all this aroused the envy (*invidia*, a word which recurs throughout the *Hist. Cal.* being, of course, the same as that used in the Vulgate of the enemies of Christ) of his rivals and they complained that 'all the world has gone after him' (Luke 16:3). 'We have gained nothing by persecuting him,' they said, 'only increased his fame. We meant to extinguish the light of his name but all we have done is to make it shine still brighter.' (*H. C.*, p. 90.)

This was clearly an impressive period, but to sustain it would have required the kind of virtues Abelard had never developed—summed up for the monk in the one word: stability. And so, full of fears for the persecutions he thought were being directed against him ('God is my witness that I never heard that an assembly of ecclesiastics had met without thinking this was convened to condemn me.' (*H. C.*, p. 93)), combined with his apparent inability to control his disorderly students (*H. C.*, p. 94, n. 1), he accepted the abbacy of St. Gildas de Rhuys, some 360 miles away in a wild spot on the west coast of Brittany. Thus he exchanged a difficult but fruitful situation for an impossible and barren one; disorderly but devoted students for disorderly and murderous monks.

However, the ill wind which blew Abelard to Brittany enabled him two years later in 1128 to house Heloise, and those of her nuns who remained with her, at the Paraclete when Suger, now abbot of Saint-Denis, claimed the convent at Argenteuil as the property of that monastery. The contact—the first for ten years—between Abelard and Heloise during these negotiations seems to have been entirely impersonal, it never occurring to Abelard that Heloise's feelings had not been stifled with his own which, if one were able to gauge such things, would surely provide an all-time record of the effect of self-pity on the imagination. But a few years later in 1132, while still at St. Gildas, Abelard wrote the *Historia* and a copy came into Heloise's hands. In consequence she took up her pen and re-opened the relationship in a manner calculated to pierce even Abelard's self-absorption. Having succeeded in the course of two extremely personal letters in gaining his full attention—or, at least, very much more of it than he normally spared from himself—she held it, and the efforts she put him to on behalf of herself and her community are the best, in the sense of being the least egotistical and most disinterested, he ever made. At her request he poured out hymns and sermons and advice in abundance, and his Rule for the Paraclete has some fine passages in it and shows an intimate knowledge of monastic life, even if the tedious tenor of its style would hardly inspire anyone to live it.

After Heloise's installation as abbess of the Paraclete, Bernard went there to preach, the Paraclete being not far from Clairvaux. Heloise told Abelard that Bernard was more like an angel than a man but reported privately that Bernard had criticized their use of Matthew's version of the Lord's Prayer instead of, as was then customary, the Lucan version. Abelard rose to this criticism with his usual heat and wrote Bernard a letter in which he argued an excellent case in favour of the Matthean version concluding with: 'Whoever he be let him notice that use is not to be preferred to reason nor custom to truth'[10]—a saying Abelard often repeats and which conveys briefly both the appeal and the limitation of his thought.

There is no further record of direct contact between Abelard and Bernard until 1138 when William of St. Thierry aroused Bernard with an anguished letter written as a result of reading Abelard's *Introductio ad theologiam* and *Theologia christiana* which a novice had brought with him to William's monastery at Signy. Abelard, meanwhile, had gained release from his abbey of St. Gildas but with the right to retain the rank of abbot, and in these last few years, through a mixture of stretches of teaching in Paris combined with stretches of disappearance (which in a more esoteric character would lend themselves to speculations), had acquired immense prestige. So William writes: 'Fear lest we offend a man of standing drives from our hearts the fear of offending God'[11] —which, of course, effectively engaged Bernard in battle.

After some preliminary and apparently amicable skirmishes between Bernard and Abelard it became clear that Abelard had no intention of modifying his views in accordance with Bernard's requirements. Bernard then preached against Abelard and Abelard retaliated by challenging Bernard to a confrontation, not doubting that in debate he could confound the Abbot of Clairvaux. It seems that Bernard also expected to be confounded, and the view generally held at the present time is that Bernard's reluctance to meet Abelard in open debate was due to his sense of being out of his depth in the face of Abelard's greater dialectical skill. But if a dog challenges an elephant to a swimming contest in a stretch of water which at no point rises higher than the elephant's knees can the elephant be said to be out of his depth because he cannot swim in it? And this analogy precisely conveys the frustration the intuitive man feels in relation to the logical man, and would alone account for Bernard's excitement—although in a longer study it would be interesting to explore other possibilities.

Abelard chose a great public occasion to meet Bernard—a solemn exposition of relics at Sens in the presence of the King of France and most of the bishops—and arrived for it surrounded by disciples, the principal one at this time being Arnald of Brescia. Arnald, under the guise of extreme austerity of life, was a particularly nasty rabble-rouser who had lately been expelled from his own country but was destined to return there and, after many years of successful terrorism in Rome, to be hanged. That Abelard should have been yoked to a man whose career and character were alike repellent is significant and suggests something of that interior disintegration which was about to be revealed.

Bernard brought nineteen charges against Abelard,[12] a large number of which Abelard could easily have sported with for as long as anyone remained interested. Instead he was suddenly speechless in that great assembly, like the man who had not on a wedding garment (Matt. 22:11-14). The intellectual structure he had built up was unexpectedly shown to be hollow as it collapsed in the face of Bernard's fullness of heart and mind. Spiritual sterility challenged spiritual fecundity, and was ashamed because he had no children to speak with his enemies in the gate (Ps. 127).

And so Abelard, unable to utter a word in his own defence, was condemned. For a brief account of the last lap, Knowles cannot be bettered:

> He appealed to Rome, and set out for the threshold of the Apostles, preceded by a bunch of the fiercest and most devastating letters ever written by St. Bernard, but was intercepted on the road by Peter the Venerable, abbot of Cluny, who received him with characteristic sympathy, gave him a home in his own great abbey, and advised him to retract what was clearly erroneous or rash in his teaching. Abelard, with what searchings of heart we know not, took the wise if unexpected decision to follow this advice, and at a meeting with St. Bernard complete harmony was established in personal relations, though Abelard's retractation stopped at the minimum possible, while in a final apologia he gave the abbot of Clairvaux as good as he had received. Back at Cluny, well over sixty and an invalid, he was still active as a writer. He had been condemned by the pope, but Peter, furnished with his retractation, obtained permission for him to remain undisturbed at Cluny. His last year was a surprising and moving contrast to his earlier life; he lived in submission and simplicity till April 1142, when he died in peace in a priory of Cluny at Châlon-sur-Saône. It was then that Peter the Venerable wrote to Heloise that most remarkable letter in which, besides expressing his admiration for herself and Abelard, he refers to their old association and anticipates their reunion beyond the tomb, 'where, beyond these voices, there is peace.'[13]

* * * * *

At the time of writing the only works of Abelard's available in English are his *Ethics*, the *Historia Calamitatum* and the correspondence with Heloise. But translators are doubtless working on the rest and it will not be too long, one supposes, before there is a single volume entitled 'The Complete Works of Peter Abelard'. It will include less than a dozen works, most of them relatively short treatises, the more important being *De Unitate et Trinitate Divina*, the work condemned at Soissons; and the three from which the nineteen *capitula* were taken and condemned at Sens: *Introductio ad theologiam*, *Theologia christiana*, and *Epitome theologia christiana*. It will also include the collection of contradictory sayings from Scripture and the Fathers, *Sic et Non*; and a number of slighter treatises such as the *Dialogue between the Christian, the Philosopher and the Jew* and the *Commentary on Romans*, as well as those works in translation already mentioned.

Of Abelard's theological treatises, which landed him in so much trouble, Southern says the earliest version, condemned at Soissons, 'is the sharpest and best and shows what he really thought'.[14] Thereafter he amended and qualified and tried, with his usual desire to have things both ways, to express his opinions in forms at once orthodox and alarming. That is, he hoped to upset orthodox opinion but without giving orthodox opinion any grounds for upsetting him in return. As these tactics have been brought to a point of refinement among professional theologians in our day it is hard for us to share the excitement Abelard aroused for, in comparison, he looks like a veritable beginner at the business—which, of course, historically, is exactly what he was.

Of his other works, *Sic et Non* seems to have generated the most friction. 'Even now', Southern says, 'there is something shocking about flinging down so large a body of contradictions without any attempt to reconcile them.'[15] Déchanet on the other hand—and he is not the only one—calls it 'that great book'[16] which, however, seems to be a judgement urged rather by the current compulsion to over-rate Abelard than by any intrinsic merit in the work. This compulsion is shown most clearly by Luscombe at the end of his otherwise excellent introduction to the *Ethics*, which is called—or rather, miscalled, since there is nothing in it likely to contribute to that end—*Know Thyself*. 'The text itself', writes Luscombe, 'is bracing and exciting in its argumentation [and] also somewhat spicy, for Abelard had a vivid sexual imagination.' (No doubt this is intended to encourage the reader to endure the tediousness of reading Abelard himself.) 'Moreover,' continues Luscombe (in case it does not), 'Abelard did not mince words when expressing his dissatisfaction with the quality of the prelates of his own day or with the contemporary nobility. In this way his work leads us back from the task of speculation and of introspection to the reappraisal of the real world of practical and social endeavour.'[17] Since *Know Thyself* seems to consist of series of barren speculations on unlikely contingencies ('For example,' writes Abelard, 'if someone compels a Religious who is bound in chains to lie between women and if he is brought to pleasure, not to consent, by the softness of the bed and through contact with the women, who may presume . . .' and so on) one can only ask: to which 'real world' does Professor Luscombe refer?

It is possible that if one were to read all Abelard's works he would emerge in a light more commensurate with the praise he is at present receiving. But it is more likely that when his entire output can be seen whole it will become impossible to continue blowing him up and that he will then subside into a suitable place among the world's tenth-rate thinkers. Leaving aside his role in the development of Scholasticism has he, then, any real importance? In the Letters of Direction to Heloise, Abelard quotes a beautiful passage from Origen which sums up his own view of his role:

> Those wells which the Philistines had filled with earth are surely men who close their spiritual understanding, so that they neither drink themselves nor allow others to drink. Hear the word of the Lord: 'Alas for you lawyers and Pharisees! You have taken away the key of knowledge; you did not go in yourselves, and did not permit those who wished to enter.' But let us never cease from digging wells of living water, and by discussing new things as well as old, let us make ourselves like the teacher of the law in the Gospel of whom the Lord said that he could 'produce from his store both old and new.' Let us return to Isaac and dig with him wells of living water, even if the Philistines obstruct us; even if they use violence, let us carry on with our well-digging, so that to us too it may be said: 'Drink water from your own cisterns and your own wells.' And let us dig until our wells overflow with water in our courtyards, so that our knowledge of the Scriptures is not only sufficient for ourselves, but we can teach others and show them how to drink.[18]

The disparity between Origen and Abelard is as great as it could be (although Abelard desired to be Origen's peer), and yet there is a sense in which Abelard was right in feeling that his function was to oppose the forces of philistinism. The Philistines provide recurring occasions of conflict in the Church and have to be resisted in every generation. So it is not the necessity of digging afresh the wells of living water or of issuing forth against Goliath which is in question but the character of the man who takes upon himself these tasks. This brings us to a consideration of Abelard's one work, the *Historia Calamitatum*, which, for real interest, is a brilliant exception to all the rest.

Attempts in autobiography were beginning to be made at this time, a fact which in itself indicates man's radically altered attention, but Abelard's was unique and marked a new development in introspection. Its original title was 'Abelard's letter of consolation to his friend', and although this may have been a conventional device, given Abelard's desire to improve upon every situation, it is quite likely that he used the misfortunes of an actual friend as a springboard for recounting his own. In any event, it is written in a style—although in accordance with the conventions of the times—more likely to arouse wrath than assuage grief ('In comparison with my trials you will see that your own are nothing, or only slight, and will find them easier to bear.' *H.C.*, p. 57) and the recipient, if he existed, doubtless felt on reading it that a letter of consolation from Abelard ranked fairly high in comparison with Abelard's trials.

The account, which takes Abelard up to his early fifties when, it appears, he was still Abbot of St. Gildas, is written in a vivid, compressed style which, together with its selectivity—it amounts to less than fifty pages in translation—makes every line contributory to the total effect. The immediate aim seems to be a desire to forestall further criticism by supplying abundant material for it and then getting in first. The ultimate aim is more mysterious. For there is a compelling quality about the *Historia Calamitatum* which raises it to a level above ordinary interpretation and justifies attempts to see in it something of universal significance. And this compelling quality is due, I believe, to it being an inspired work and Abelard its unconscious but wholly appropriate vehicle. Abelard is compelled to reveal, for 'those who have ears to hear', the whole psychology of spiritual sterility.

That, at any rate, is my view. But it is worth noting a more sympathetic one. Mary McLaughlin, in her article 'Abelard as Autobiographer: The Motives and Meaning of his *Story of Calamities*', has written:

> Sharing with Luther and Kierkegaard, among others, a passion for describing and expressing his sufferings, he seems to belong with them to the company of those reformers and innovators whose personal sufferings and struggles have a public significance, who are destined not only to participate actively in, but to endure and articulate in their extreme forms, certain crucial experiences and transformations of their times. Impelled, whether consciously or not, to take on the most arduous tasks of their societies, such men are commonly possessed by

a sense of vocation or mission that is a major source of their peculiarly symbiotic relationships with the larger movements of their times. In Abelard's case, as in others of this kind, the sense of a special calling appears to have developed early, and it was to become central to his later efforts at self-definition.[19]

This is magnificently expressed and captures a vital truth about Abelard. In fact, on looking into it, there is much to disagree with. Abelard was not, it is now seen, either a reformer or an innovator. He was a popularizer of rising trends. Southern calls him a 'brilliant meteoric irritant in a period of disarray in medieval thought before the consolidation of the mid-twelfth century'.[20] And Poole, in a rare moment of sober estimate, confines Abelard to the status of being 'first and foremost a critic' and goes on: 'The love of opposition was his normal stimulus to production; and the fact that the object of his attack held one view led him inevitably to emphasize the contrary.'[21] Likewise it is difficult to share Mary McLaughlin's grand view of the sufferings of a man in whom feeling was confined to self-pity. Nevertheless it is true that his personal sufferings had a public significance and that he had to endure and articulate certain crucial experiences which expressed the transformations of the times. But that was because, in taking on the arduous tasks of his society, he showed himself to be not so much an Isaac or a David as another Goliath, arrogant and certain of his invincibility, whose presumption ('Ye have heard that it hath been said by them of old time ... But *I* say ...' was Abelard's chief line) rendered him impotent in relation to life and finally drew out a true David against him. That the true David is generally regarded nowadays as the leader of the Philistines is itself a philistine verdict and belongs peculiarly to that combination of romanticism and rationalism which, as I noted at the beginning, emerged in the nineteenth century, producing a type of thinker for whom Abelard provided, and continues to provide, a welcome relief from the implications of real thought—that is, of thought which has its roots in the heart.

'AS FAR AS THOUGHT CAN REACH'

This is the title of the last part of Shaw's play *Back to Methuselah* and a critic, using it to comment on Shaw himself wrote: 'It is not very far; for thought is the formulation of feeling, and where feeling has been stifled thought has little to work on.'[22] That was precisely Abelard's case. The comment could also be applied to Bertrand Russell—to whom Southern likens Abelard—and both Shaw and Russell are typical of that climate of thought which rescued Abelard from the obscurity into which he fell after his death (being remembered through the centuries chiefly for the drama with Heloise), and which rapturously hailed him as a herald of enlightenment and the first apostle of free thought. Abelard had to wait for recognition until an era compatible with his character, and although the view of him as a free thinker broke down under the first dispassionate examination of it, we are still, psychologically, in the same era. What, then, does that suggest to us about it?

In the section called 'The emergence of modern man' we saw the change in direction of man's attention from God to himself which occurred on entering the present millenium, and the division, after Anselm, between spiritual growth—represented by Bernard—and technological and intellectual growth—represented by Abelard—and their independent development. This division between spiritual and intellectual growth is peculiar to Latin Christendom. It did not occur in Greek Christendom,[23] and it is significant that the final schism between Latin and Greek Christendom actually took place in those years (the date usually given is 1054) when in the West spirituality and theology began to fall apart.

It is, moreover, further significant that Abelard was the first to use this word theology in the sense now current in all European countries, that is, in the sense of being separate from spirituality.[24] But this separation did not, as it were, come to full harvest until the last century when the long chain of cause and effect culminated in a final shift. Whereas the 'triumph of Anselm's analytical introspective method' had been to discover God on looking into himself, man now discovered man on looking into himself, and no longer as 'bearing within himself a feeble image of the ineffable prototype', in Gregory of Sinai's words, but as being—via the apes—the peak of the evolutionary process. Since then man has been falling apart at a tremendous pace until it is no longer possible to say what the divisions are. 'Any day now I expect one of my students will hand in an essay beginning: "Many mathematicicians feel that two and two make four"', an article in *The Times* began recently. And the writer went on to say that the word 'feels' is now being used to do duty for 'believes', 'holds', 'is convinced', 'claims'—almost 'knows'. Reason, apparently, is a bourgeois illusion, and Nietzsche, Marx, and Freud between them have rendered appeal to it vain.[25]

So the problem is no longer that of the exaltation of reason divorced from feeling but of the fragmentation and confusion of both divorced from their Source of unity. And this was what Bernard foresaw, as Pieper says in his book, *Scholasticism*:

> Bernard's passionate and truly 'philosophical' interest was entirely directed toward full 'realization,' toward existential Wholeness, which is to say 'salvation'. And he regarded all forms of human expression, his philosophising as well as his theology, as designed to serve that Whole. It was precisely this kind of salvation that Bernard considered to be endangered and undermined by 'dialecticians' of the type of Abelard. The danger which he quite rightly saw dawning in such personalities, and which he fought with all his might, was nothing less than this: that the substance of Truth, by which living man is nourished, would be consumed by an empty formalism of 'correct' thinking—consumed and reduced to vanishing point.[26]

If we look at the heirs of Abelard—very much in the ascendance in academic circles—we see that we have arrived at that vanishing point, for the present function of theology seems largely to consist in telling us what it is no longer possible—or 'correct'—to believe. On reading, for instance, *The Remaking of Christian Doctrine*, one is left with the impression that the author—as one might expect in this technological age—possesses a magic 'disappearing' aerosol spray (one puff for the Atonement; puff, puff for the Incarnation; puff, puff, puff—and that was the Trinity that was!); while another, equally symptomatic, book by an Oxbridge theologian, recently published, has been described by one critic as '£5.00's worth of hesitation'. Such nervy agnosticism starts back in dismay from the vitality and assurance of a Bernard:

> Far be it from us, then, to suppose that the Christian faith has as its boundaries those opinions of the Academicians, whose boast it is they doubt of everything and know nothing. But I for my part walk securely . . . and I know I shall not be confounded.[27]

And yet I am bound to say that my conclusion on reading *The Remaking of Christian Doctrine*[28] was rather to make me concerned about monasticism: 'Of course, this kind of theologizing is wrong, but we have only ourselves to blame for it' I thought, borrowing from the remark made about Luther by the pope of his time. Which brings me to the one division which can, I think, illuminate our understanding of what has been happening in this 'yesterday' of a thousand years, and that is the division between 'personality' and 'being' which I see as having first manifested itself in permanent contrast in the figures of Bernard and Abelard.

First it is necessary to define the terms. I understand 'personality' in its sense of being derived from *persona*—as once applied to the masks worn by actors—and the sense in which it is used in psychology. Ouspensky, in his book *In Search of the Miraculous*, says of it:

> Personality in man is what is 'not his own'. 'Not his own' means what has come from outside, what he has learned, or reflects, all traces of exterior impressions left in the memory and in the sensations, all words and movements that have been learned, all feelings created by imitation— all this is 'not his own', all this is personality ... A small child has no personality as yet. He is what he really is ... His desires, tastes, likes, dislikes, express his being—such as it is ... Culture creates personality and is at the same time the product and the result of personality. We do not realise that the whole of our life, all we call civilization, all we call science, philosophy, art and politics, is created by people's personality, that is, by what is 'not their own' in them. The element that is 'not his own' differs from what is man's 'own' by the fact that it can be lost, altered, or taken away by artificial means.[29]

That which is a man's own is, of course, his 'being' or 'essence' as Ouspensky calls it here:

> In proportion as personality grows, essence manifests itself more and more rarely and more and more feebly, and it often happens that essence stops in its growth at a very early age and grows no further ... so that the essence of a grown-up man, even that of a very intellectual and, in the accepted meaning of the word, highly 'educated' man, stops on the level of a child of five or six ... Sometimes, though very seldom, and sometimes when it is least expected, essence proves fully grown and fully developed in a man, even in cases of undeveloped personality, and in this case essence unites together everything that is serious and real in a man. But this happens very seldom. As a rule a man's essence is either

primitive, savage, and childish, or else simply stupid. The development of essence depends on work on oneself. A very important moment in the work on oneself is when a man begins to distinguish between his personality and his essence . . . But in order to enable essence to grow up, it is first of all necessary to weaken the constant pressure of personality upon it, because the obstacles to the growth of essence are contained in personality.[30]

This weakening of the constant pressure of personality on essence, or being, so that it may grow, is the function of the monastic life. It provides—or should provide—the means by which there may be created in a person that which is his 'own', is indestructible and cannot be 'lost, altered, or taken away'. 'Your joy no man taketh from you.' (John 16:22.) And for this the one thing necessary is that one is not much cumbered about with personality, even in the service of God, for it is as easy to get stuck in personality in relation to God as it is easy to get stuck in it in relation to the world. Monastic discipline, then, is designed to break up the crystallization of personality—whatever form it may have taken. And in the Cistercian tradition, in particular, *lectio divina*, as we have seen, forms a large part of that discipline. For, if the distinction between being and personality is understood it can also be understood that all Scripture is written i) from the standpoint of being, ii) by men whose being is united to the Being of God, and iii) for men who desire to be united in their being with the Being of God. And from the standpoint of being every word of Scripture is true.

All this is not to say that personality is 'bad' and being is 'good'. Personality is necessary; should, indeed, be the faithful servant of being, while hell, no less than heaven, is inhabited by people of being since only being can survive the shock of death. In what sense, then, does it strike me that the results of personality cut off from being—as manifested today in much theology and biblical criticism—can be charged to the account of monasticism? Writing on Bernard, Knowles has an interesting passage which relates to this point:

> It would be unpardonable, in glancing at the various intellectual currents of the twelfth century, to omit all reference to the dynamic personality of one who, though never precisely a teacher of the schools, was capable, alone of all his contemporaries, of drowning or, if the expression be allowed, of 'jamming' all other voices, and who, on the

great web of medieval religious thought and sentiment, changed and formed more patterns than any other man of his century. It is at first sight a paradox that one who, when all is said and done, affected his contemporaries more universally and more profoundly than any of those we have mentioned in the last two chapters, should stand entirely apart from, and should in some ways be positively hostile to, learning of all kinds. In many ways, indeed, the reputation of St. Bernard for ferocious mental puritanism is the outcome of a piece of supreme, if unconscious, bluff. Historians and critics have been so occupied in registering their disapproval and framing replies to Bernard's attack on the wordy volubility of philosophers and worldly wisdom that teaches only vanity, or in admiring his profession that his only learning is the cross of Christ, that they have failed to note that they have to deal, not only with a speculative theologian of wide reading and great intellectual power, but with a literary genius of the first order, the greatest master of language in the Middle Ages who, alone of all this age, has a power equal to that of Demosthenes, of Cicero and of Burke, to carry us with him on the gale of his eloquence . . .[31]

As this quotation from Knowles reminds us, although it is right to see a great and deep conflict between Bernard and Abelard, the monasteries and the schools, the claims of contemplation and the demands of the discursive intellect, or, in the terms I have been using, between being and personality, it can be misleading. For while Abelard belongs wholly to one side of the dichotomy, Bernard would dwarf him on either side. The pupil of Saint-Vorles towers above his opponents in the schools. Here is a man with a personality developed beyond anything that Abelard, cramped by conceit and self-concern, could show; a man who could beat the schools hollow at their own game *and yet* who threw his genius, his personality, on to the side of being, not on to the side that would have seemed most to foster it. To be detached from personality is a great thing; to be detached from such a personality is sanctity of the highest order. No wonder Dante finds Bernard to introduce him to the highest sphere of heaven—the Empyrean:

> . . . tale era io mirando la vivace
> carità di colui, che in questo mondo,
> contemplando, gustò di quella pace.

> (. . . such was I, gazing upon the living
> love of him who in this world by
> contemplation tasted of that peace.)[32]

So, Bernard threw the whole weight of his amazing personality on to the side of being. But was he right? Did he force a wedge between personality and being, thought and feeling, theology and spirituality which without him—notwithstanding Abelard and all he represented—might have retained their true relationship? And did he thus deprive monasticism of its capacity to generate real thought by limiting it to an affective way based wholly on the development of being to the exclusion of personality? And did he thereby promote a compartmentalization which on the one hand left being without proper expression and on the other paved the way for that kind of thought which fails to reach far because it issues only from itself and so, inevitably, becomes increasingly disincarnate and narcissistic?

It seems there is a sense in which one must answer yes. For while there are religious in whom personality remains paramount, and academicians in whom being is fully developed, the division between thought and feeling which manifested itself in Bernard has led, generally speaking, to a division between the contemplative and the intellectual life—so impoverishing both. In that light the great men of the next century—Dominic, Thomas Aquinas, Bonaventura, and many others—can be seen as drawing them together again, while in the intervening centuries there are many examples of men and movements that have achieved the primacy of being while using personality to further its ends. But such men and movements represent, it seems to me, the repairing of a break—a break all too ready to fall apart again, resulting on one side in an oppressive over-emphasis on being and on the other in the development of personality at the expense of being. In our day the reaction in monasticism to an over-emphasis on being is to allow personality enough rope with which to hang itself—which it undoubtedly will, and monasticism along with it, if the means necessary for the development of being cease to be understood. Equally there are signs in the rising generation of a reaction against living in personality, and if that is true then a development radically different from that of the last thousand years is, literally, coming into being.

Bernard has been called the 'last of the Fathers' and the negative significance of this title may be that after him the capacity to understand the Bible from the standpoint of being became exceptional instead of the norm. As a result, due to the tireless activity of personality—especially from Darwin onwards—the pass has now been reached where even in a monastic milieu what is called, with pejorative overtones, a 'spiritual interpretation' is hardly, if at all, tolerated.

But even if Bernard's influence can be seen as in some sense disastrous (and those whom God appoints to mediate his will always are, humanly speaking, in some sense disastrous; Darwin, just referred to, is another such example) we still, I believe, need him as much as ever, even if we must ask questions about, and attempt answers to, the problem he has left with us. For he understood the 'one thing necessary' with a marvellous clarity and urgency—no less urgent now than when he wrote:

> There are two dangers that we must guard against. We must not give to others what we have received for ourselves; nor must we keep for ourselves that which we have received to spend on others. You fall into the latter error if you possess the gift of eloquence or wisdom and yet—through fear or sloth or false humility—neglect to use the gift for others' benefit. And, on the other hand, you dissipate and lose what is your own if, without right intention and from some wrong motive, you hasten to outpour yourself on others when your own soul is only half-filled.
>
> If you are wise, therefore, you will show yourself a tank and not a pipe. For a pipe pours out as fast as it takes in; but a tank waits till it is full before it overflows, and so communicates its surplus without loss to itself. We have all too few such tanks in the Church at present, though we have pipes in plenty. Of so great charity are those who mediate the heavenly waters to us that they desire to pour out when they themselves have not been inpoured; they are readier to speak than to listen, eager to teach that which they do not know, and most anxious to exercise authority on others although they have not learnt to rule themselves! . . . But thou, my brother, whose own salvation is hardly yet assured, whose charity is feeble and unstable, if it exists at all, thou must learn not to give except when thou art full . . . Be filled thyself. Then—but discreetly, mind—pour out of thy fullness. Charity, which is thus discreet as well as generous, does not waste itself by giving out but rather gains in depth . . . So you see with what great graces we need to be inpoured before we venture to give out to others—if indeed our self-giving is to be out of our fullness, not our poverty! First, we need compunction; then devotion; thirdly, the travail of repentance; fourthly, good

works; fifthly, faithful prayer; sixthly, leisure for contemplation; and, in the seventh place, the fullness of love. All these things are the work in us of one and the same Spirit, according to the operation that we have called infusion; to the end that the other, which is called effusion, may be exercised with purity of heart—and therefore safely—to the praise and glory of our Lord Jesus Christ, who with the Father and the Holy Spirit liveth and reigneth, God to the ages of ages. Amen.[33]

* * * * * *

ACKNOWLEDGEMENTS

We are greatly indebted to the generosity of Mrs. Radice and to Penguin Books Ltd. for allowing us to quote extensively from *The Letters of Abelard and Heloise*, translated by Betty Radice and first published in Penguin Classics in 1974.

Permission to use the following extracts has also been sought and kindly given:

Two passages from *Medieval Humanism and Other Studies* by R. W. Southern, by permission of Basil Blackwell, Oxford.

Two passages from *The Evolution of Medieval Thought* by David Knowles, by permission of the Longman Group Limited.

The passage from *The Mystical Theology of Saint Bernard* by Etienne Gilson, by permission of Sheed and Ward Limited.

Two passages from *Saint Bernard on the Song of Songs*, translated by a Religious C.S.M.V., by permission of A. R. Mowbray Limited.

NOTES TO PART 1

1. *The Letters of Abelard and Heloise*, translated and with an Introduction by Betty Radice, Penguin Classics, 1974, p. 42. I have relied heavily on the excellent introduction and the notes to the text throughout the book.
2. *Saint Bernard of Clairvaux* by Bruno Scott James, London 1957, p. 139.
3. cf. *The Evolution of Medieval Thought* by David Knowles, Longmans 1962, p. 79.
4. *Medieval Humanism and Other Studies* by R. W. Southern, Harper Torchbook, 1970, p. 35. The essay 'Medieval Humanism' brilliantly illuminates the subject and remains for me by far the best work I have read on it.
5. Ibid. pp. 32 f. 6. Ibid. p. 33. 7. Ibid. p. 34.

8. *Nature, Man and Society in the Twelfth Century* by M-D. Chenu O.P., University of Chicago Press, 1968, pp.43-45.
9. *Ev. of Med. Thought* (see n.3) p.147.
10. *Historia Calamitatum* in *The Letters of Abelard and Heloise* (see n.1), pp.57-58. All references to the *Hist. Cal.* are to Betty Radice's translation and from this point on will be incorporated in the text, abbreviated as follows: *H.C.* pp.57-58.
11. *Gislebertus: Sculptor of Autun* by Denis Grivot and George Zarnecki, Orion Press, New York, 1961, p.77.
12. *Vita Prima Bernardi*, translated by Geoffrey Webb and Adrian Walker, A.R. Mowbray, 1960, p.20.
13. Quoted by Bruno Scott James (see n.2), p.23.
14. *Vita Prima*, p.24. 15. Ibid. p.25.
16. St Stephen Harding, the remarkable Englishman who helped to found Cîteaux, and framed the Cistercian constitution, was the abbot at this time. It is likely, in fact, that he was aware of the approaching invasion, for Bernard's fame as a recruiting agent for Cîteaux became such that, according to the *Vita Prima*, 'mothers hid their sons when Bernard came near, and wives clung to their husbands . . .' (p.32)
17. See next note.
18. From the chapter 'Schola Caritatis' in *The Mystical Theology of Saint Bernard* by Etienne Gilson, Sheed and Ward, 1940, pp. 60 ff.
19. From the chapter 'The Revival of Dialectic' in *Ev. of Med. Thought*, p.93.
20. This is, of course, an immense over-simplification. In fact the structure and character of twelfth-century society was rigidly Judaic. Neither is it possible to confine even the individual to one type or another. Abelard himself exemplifies the situation: an Aristotelian 'Greek' in regard to ideas; a 'Jew' in regard to morality. Abbot Suger, on the other hand, might be said to have been an Aristotelian at the practical level, a Platonist at the aesthetic level and, finally (after his conversion under the influence of St Bernard), a Jew at the spiritual level. Nevertheless, the simplification, I think, stands, and suggests why someone like Rupert of Deutz, a biblical mystic on the Hebraic side, although involved in a number of central controversies, made no impression on the times and felt himself to be out of tune with them.
21. *Saint Bernard on the Song of Songs*, translated and edited by a Religious of C.S.M.V., A.R. Mowbray, 1952, pp. 107 f. (Sermon 36).
22. In a course of lectures, 'Abelard, his friends and his enemies', given by R.W. Southern in Oxford, 1975, Southern presented a view of Anselm of Laon as a revolutionary who succeeded by virtue of his dullness in introducing the study of the Bible into the secular curriculum—a view which was itself revolutionary. This suggests that Anselm's rage with Abelard was due not to jealousy—as Abelard

inevitably thought—but to his fear that Abelard's provocative handling of the new method would jeopardise what he, Anselm, had carefully rendered safe over many years of patient work. But Anselm had had a long run on a low light, so to speak, and it was inevitable that an Abelard should emerge from the pot to blow the lid off. Southern concluded his lectures by saying that Abelard's 'chief service was that he drew on himself all the hostility directed at the whole scholastic enterprise.'

I am deeply indebted to Sister Benedicta SLG for the detailed notes she took of these lectures on my behalf. I have referred to them constantly.

NOTES TO PART II

1. A. Victor Murray, *Abelard and Saint Bernard*, Manchester University Press, 1967, p. 9.

2. *Rule of St. Benedict*, edited and translated by Justin McCann, London, 1952, pp. 7 and 11.

3. See Jean Leclercq's *The Love of Learning and the Desire for God*, a study of monastic culture, for the monk's attitude to *lectio* and *meditatio*. Fordham University Press, New York, 1961.

4. 'Treatise against Abelard' (Letter 190), *Life and Works of Saint Bernard*, translated by S.J. Eales, London, 1896, Vol. II, p. 583.

5. Ibid.

6. Letter 4: Abelard to Heloise in the *Letters of Abelard and Heloise* (see n.1/I) p. 147. Further references to these letters will be incorporated in the text, abbreviated as follows: L.4, p. 147.

7. In fact, Eusebius's story of Origen's self-mutilation is now regarded sceptically by some scholars. See H. Chadwick, *Early Christian Thought and the Classical Tradition*, pp. 67f. and notes. The evidence from Origen is against it. In his *Commentary on Matthew* (XV.1-5) he discusses the passage about eunuchs and is concerned that it should not be taken literally. The only knife Origen will tolerate is the spiritual knife, namely, the Word: 'Those who receive the "living and active Word, sharper than any two-edged sword", as the apostle says, and cuts off his concupiscence, not touching his body, and makes himself thus, not because of the praise of men, or fear of them, but only because of the hope of the heavenly kingdom—these are they who have made themselves eunuchs for the sake of the kingdom of God.' But Abelard did not, apparently, read Greek, and the Latin translation of the *Comm. on Matt.* is selective and does not include Origen's discussion on self-emasculation. (I am indebted to Andrew Louth for the information in this note.)

8. 'Modern Psychology and the Interpretation of Medieval Texts' by Jean Leclercq, OSB in *Speculum*, Vol. XLVIII, No. 3, July 1973, p. 484. But see also Southern's essay 'The Letters of Abelard and Heloise' in *Medieval Humanism*. Easily the best account.

9. This is not to say that Heloise was all white and Abelard all black. They were a finely matched pair. One could even make a case for Abelard being more in love with Heloise than she with him. She was, I think, largely sustained in her tragedy by being a terrific role player and by the incomparable advantage of being devoid of humour. Indeed, had there been a flicker of humour in her make-up Abelard would undoubtedly have dropped her like a hot brick in the first round and we would never have heard of her. The immense seriousness with which she recognized it was essential to take him must have had its counterpart in her attitude towards herself.
One should mention—and a footnote seems an appropriate place—that Heloise and Abelard had a son called, by Heloise, Astrolabe.
One's awareness of the authenticity discussions should also be noted. But if the psychological authenticity of the letters between Heloise and Abelard is understood further discussion can only seem a waste of time.

10. Quoted in A. Victor Murray, *Abelard and St. Bernard*, p. 35.

11. The text of this letter is given almost in full in Déchanet's valuable book, *William of St. Thierry*, Cistercian Publications, Spencer, Mass., 1972, p. 55. Approaching Abelard through William of St. Thierry is far more instructive than approaching him through Bernard, and I regret that lack of space prevented me pursuing that line here.

12. For a short and really comprehensible account of the *capitula* see Edward Little, 'Bernard and Abelard at the Council of Sens, 1140' in *Bernard of Clairvaux*: Studies presented to Dom Jean Leclercq, Cistercian Publications, Washington, 1973, pp. 55-71. For a longer study see *Abelard and St. Bernard*, A. Victor Murray.

13. *Ev. of Med. Thought*, p. 120.

14. Lectures on 'Abelard, his friends and his enemies'. See n.22/I.

15. Ibid.

16. *William of St. Thierry*, p. 4.

17. *Peter Abelard's Ethics*, edited and translated by D.E. Luscombe, Clarendon Press, 1971, p. xxxvii.

18. *The Letters of Abelard and Heloise*, Betty Radice, p. 267.

19. *Speculum*, Vol. XLII, 1967, pp. 463-488.

20. Lectures—see n. 14 above.

21. *Illustrations of the History of Medieval Thought and Learning* by R.L. Poole, first published in 1884. This edition, New York, 1960, p. 140.

22. Hugh Kingsmill, *The Progress of a Biographer*, London, 1949, p. 48.

23. Or rather, one should say, it did not occur in the same way. The division in Greek Christendom has been—far more intensely than in the West—between the 'Jew' and the 'Greek' psychologies. But whereas in the West the Greek side has tended to degenerate into a barren intellectualism, in the East spiritual power has been maintained in both camps. Another over-simplification, of course, but all there is space for.

24. See Knowles, *Ev. of Med. Thought*, p. 126.

25. 'The Struggle for the Vindication of Reason' by Anthony Hanson, 8 May 1976.

26. Op. cit. Faber and Faber, 1961, p. 90.

27. 'Treatise against Abelard', ed. cit. p. 575.

28. I am fully aware that Maurice Wiles represents only a strand in current theology. But, like Abelard, he symbolizes a state of affairs—Abelard at one end and Wiles at the other. And in Wiles one can see that we are again at the end of a road.

29. Op. cit. Routledge & Kegan Paul, 1950. This and the following quotation have been extracted from pp. 161-163. Ouspensky, of course, is quoting the teaching of Gurdjieff, and is quoted here in the spirit of 'despoiling the Egyptians'. This is too valuable a jewel to be left behind—even if the setting is 'wrong'.

30. See previous note.

31. *Ev. of Med. Thought*, p. 147.

32. *Paradiso*, Canto XXXI, p. 381 in the Temple Classics edition, 1899.

33. *Saint Bernard on the Song of Songs*, see n. 21/I. Extracted from pp. 44-48. I recently heard a Dominican take issue with St. Bernard on the question of being a tank, his point being that God is just as pleased with pipes. Perhaps he is!

APOPHTHEGMATA BERNARDI

SOME ASPECTS OF ST. BERNARD OF CLAIRVAUX

Sister Benedicta, SLG

BERNARD OF CLAIRVAUX has been described as 'one of the small class of supremely great men whose gifts and opportunities have been exactly matched.'[1] For forty years he made his abbey at Clairvaux the spiritual centre of Europe and both the Cistercian Order and the spirituality of western Europe were profoundly changed by his influence. He is comparable in many ways with both Augustine of Hippo and Anselm of Canterbury but though he is nearer to us in time than either of them, and though abundant material is available about him as well as by him, Bernard remains in some sense opaque and inaccessible. Like Augustine, his prolific writings are available, and like Anselm he had biographers who had known him intimately and could meet, like Eadmer with Anselm, Dr. Johnson's dictum, 'Nobody can write the life of a man but those who have eat and drunk and lived in social intercourse with him'.[2] Yet Bernard is not as immediate to us as Augustine and Anselm are. It may be because he had no contemporary biographer of the genius of Eadmer[3] and has not yet been provided with a sensitive and personal modern biography to match that of Augustine.[4]

Until such a biography appears, we must try in indirect ways to discover Bernard for ourselves. His writings and particularly his letters[5] provide the best way of doing this; the descriptions of him in the *Vita Prima* also provide some insight into his life. I would, however, like to offer here a suggestion of a minor way in which we can begin to understand Bernard, not as a spiritual giant nor in his great and public character, but as his own monks remembered him from his daily life at Clairvaux. A tradition of understanding the saints in this way was established in the fourth century among the first Christian monks in Egypt and this desert tradition was one which was familiar to the early Cistercians including Bernard.[6] The sayings of famous ascetics were remembered, often with brief and vivid anecdotes about them, by their disciples and these were collected and preserved as written records of the living teaching of these masters of the inner life. They are not so much a matter of exact historical record as glimpses of the experience of being with these men as their disciples remember it. These vivid and lively collections of sayings have been preserved as the *Apophthegmata Patrum*, or, as the West knew them, the *Verba Seniorum*.[7] Through them, it is possible to encounter the founders of monasticism in a fresh and personal way and to discover their wisdom as an immediate and relevant event, whether it is through the words of Antony the Great, 'Our life and our death is with our neighbour; if we gain our brother we have gained God',[8] or the picture of the patient Negro, Moses, entering an assembly that had met to judge a brother's faults, carrying a broken jug from which water was leaking. and saying, 'My sins run out behind me, and I am come to judge another'.[9]

There is of course no collection of *Apophthegmata Bernardi*, and it would not be possible to collect sayings of the same kind as those of the desert fathers: they are inimitable and belong to their ethos. All I want to suggest is that it is possible to gain an immediate understanding of Bernard of Clairvaux through fragments of his sayings, pictures of his actions, as they were remembered by his brothers at Clairvaux, in a way parallel to that of the communication of sanctity in the desert. There are a number of stories about Bernard which were remembered by his contemporaries and recorded a generation or so later. This is difficult material to use, most of all because it forms part of the hagiography surrounding the saint and it therefore rapidly acquired pious overtones. But it is possible to see in these brief tales Bernard caught as it were in a sudden shaft of sunlight, unaware and intensely alive, saying what was really in his heart, acting with all the passion and zeal that he had for God and towards those in contact with him. This is Bernard as his brethren agreed he had been and while this is by no means the whole picture, it provides a living context that the writings and official *Lives* lack.

Bernard entered the newly-founded Cistercian order in 1112; he was made abbot of the new foundation of Clairvaux five years later at the age of twenty-seven and he held that position until his death in 1153. He spent much time out of his monastery on the affairs of church and state and he was at Clairvaux for relatively brief periods. But Clairvaux was his home, the centre of his life and work, and it is there that the most personal recollections of him are to be found. William of St. Thierry stresses how keenly his monks felt that Bernard belonged there with them when he quotes their reply to those who wanted them to urge Bernard to undertake yet more outside work: 'We have given up all we had and we have bought the precious pearl . . . he is our precious pearl and our treasure'.[10]

As in all religious communities, stories circulated at Clairvaux about certain monks and a proportion, though not an overwhelming proportion, concerned Bernard. Herbert, a monk of Clairvaux, collected these stories and wrote them down in 1178. He knew those who had known Bernard and he collected from them their memories of the great men of the early days of the Order. Four of the stories that follow are taken from Herbert's book, *'De Miraculis'*.[11] About twenty years later another Cistercian monk, Conrad, abbot of Eberbach, began another collection of such stories in the *Exordium Magnum Cisterciense*.[12] He used Herbert's collection, with other sources, and three of the stories that follow are from his book. In both cases the stories are coloured by the ideals and prejudices of the collectors about the early days of the Order and its progress since, but there is a sense in which these incidents are still unsophisticated and immediate. They show Bernard as he appeared to those who lived with him.

There is first of all the story of Bernard as a novice under that wise and sane man, Stephen Harding; it supplements the picture of the enthusiast riding to Clairvaux at the centre of a crowd of young men kindled with his own zeal, and the serious, single-minded novice who said to himself every day, 'Bernard, what is your purpose in coming here?' and shows rather the saint in the making. The second story, told with great delicacy and simplicity, is the epitome of Bernard's prayer, and provides as deep a glimpse into the central relationship of his life as can be allowed in any way. The other stories show how the immense and burning love for God that dominated Bernard overflowed towards others: his own brothers, especially a novice caught in a depression too deep to be expressed; a brother who can only be described as the first Protestant; and the thief who became Brother Constantius.

These stories offer rare insight into the life of Bernard but what gives them depth and meaning is the underlying fact that Bernard lived what he taught: when he told Count Theobald that he would hang the thief on the cross daily, that was where his own life irrevocably hung also; when he looked through sin and condemnation to the mercy of God for his brethren, this was all he saw for himself. The Bernard of these sayings, except perhaps the first, was above all a 'man of sorrows' who was in his daily life 'acquainted with grief'. The plain fact of his severe and unremitting physical illness all his monastic life should never be forgotten in any understanding of his teaching. The fire of love which is so evident in these sayings was not a pleasant, spiritual glow, but a terrible and totally devouring flame. At the end of his life, Bernard fell silent in the intensity of that pain and love, and the final saying of his life is perhaps the most significant: 'He seemed to retire into himself concentrating all his desire on heaven; when Godfrey, bishop of Langres, came to ask his help in some matter he was surprised to find no reaction at all in Bernard who simply said, 'Do not be surprised; I am no longer of this world'.[13]

* * * * *

THE SAYINGS

1. While blessed Bernard was still a novice, every day he used to say the seven penitential psalms silently for the soul of his mother. One day he began to say these psalms after Compline and omitted some, either through carelessness or forgetfulness, went to bed and fell asleep. Abbot Stephen knew intuitively about this negligence and when he met Bernard next day he said, 'Brother Bernard, did you just abandon your psalms after Compline yesterday, or did you perhaps get someone else to say them for you?' When the young man heard this, he blushed, for he was sensitive and shy, and he prostrated himself at the abbot's feet.

(Herbert, 11, 23, col. 1332)

2. The Lord Menard, a former abbot of Mores, which is near Clairvaux, was a man renowned for piety and religious observance. He told us about a marvellous vision as if it had happened to someone else, though we thought it had happened to him. This is what he said:

> I knew a certain monk who once came upon blessed Bernard as he was praying alone in church. He lay prostrate before the altar and there appeared to be a cross on the ground before him bearing the Crucified. The blessed man was adoring and kissing it with the deepest devotion and it seemed that his Lord stretched out his arms from each side of the cross to enfold the servant of God and draw him to himself. When the monk had watched this for a while he became dazed with wonder and seemd to be beside himself. At length he turned away, lest he should offend the holy father by seeming to pry into his greatest secret if he saw him so near. So he went out silently, understanding the wonder of it and convinced that the holy man was indeed above other men in his prayer and in his life.

(Herbert 11, 19, col. 1328)

3.   Once when blessed Bernard was preaching to the brethren the Word of God, he vehemently denounced sin and put into their minds a terror of the tremendous judgement of God. He realized that some of those present were gravely disturbed in conscience and were turning towards despair. At once he was completely on fire with love for them and to the amazement of everyone he burst out with the words: 'My brothers, why are you troubled in conscience? Are the sins that you see there so great and so many that you have forgotten the inexhaustible mercy of the heart of God? In very truth I tell you, if Judas, the son of perdition, who sold and betrayed the Lord, were sitting here in this school of Christ and belonged to this Order, even he could come through repentance to forgiveness.'

(Conrad, 11, 5, p.   )

4.   Once when a solemn vigil was being celebrated, the man of God was present with his brethren. When the *Te Deum* was sung he saw many holy angels like shining lights, their faces filled with wonder at the monks' devotion. They mingled with the singers on either side of the choir, standing by them, as if rejoicing with them, and while they were singing the divine hymn with devotion the angels bustled about urging on the work in every way. From this the holy man learnt that the hymn was indeed divine and well-known to the holy angels who worked as earnestly as the monks sang devoutly.

(Conrad 11, 4, p. 101)

5.   A certain monk belonging to the holy father's community fell into such weakness of understanding by the deceits of the devil and the simplicity of his mind that he said that the bread and wine mingled with water which are placed upon the altar cannot be changed into the substance of the true body and blood of our Lord Jesus Christ. . . . The matter was referred to the venerable abbot. The monk was summoned to him and the holy abbot refuted his lack of faith according to the wisdom given to him but the monk replied, 'I cannot be persuaded by these assertions to believe that the bread and wine which are placed upon the altar are truly the body and blood of Christ and because this is so, I know that I will go to hell'. When the man of God heard this, as he always did when he found himself in a tight spot, he displayed marvellous authority: 'What', he exclaimed, 'a monk of mine go to hell? Certainly not! If you have no faith of your own, I order you, by virtue of your obedience, to go and communicate in my

faith.' Constrained by the virtue of obedience, but inwardly with no faith as it seemed to him, the monk went up to the altar and received communion. By virtue of holy obedience and by the merits of the holy father, he at once received faith in the sacrament which he preserved unabated until the day of his death.

(Conrad, 11, 6, p. 102)

6. Once when Bernard had completed the business which had taken him away from Clairvaux, he returned to the monastery and as soon as he could he went to see the novices . . . he soon had them all laughing with his easy and constructive talk, so that they would return with increased eagerness to the observance of holy obedience. But he called one of them to him and said, 'My dearest son, what is this grief that is eating your heart out?' But the novice was too abashed to say anything. So Bernard continued, 'Dearest son, I know what has been happening to you and with all the love I have for you as your father, I suffer with you. In my long absence I returned in spirit to Clairvaux . . . and I found everyone exulting in the fear of God and eager for the work of repentance; only you were sorrowful and when I saw that I sighed. I tried to draw you to me and embrace you but you turned away from me and wept bitterly so that our cowls were drenched with your tears.' When the holy father had said this, his words set the brother free from sorrow and restored him to the freedom of joy in the spirit.

(Conrad, 11, 12, pp. 106-106)

7. It once happened that the servant of God was going to see Count Theobald on business. When he drew near to the town where the Count was, he saw a large crowd of men on the road who, by order of the Count, were taking a nefarious and infamous robber away to punishment. When he saw this, the compassionate father laid his hand upon the cords that bound the wretch and said to his executioners, 'Leave this assassin to me, for I want to hang him with my own hands'. The Count was on his way to meet the man of God and when he heard this he hurried up, for he always loved and honoured Bernard with marvellous devotion. When he saw that Bernard had the rope in his hand and was leading the robber after him, he was absolutely horrified and said, 'Reverend father, whatever are you doing? Would you save a gallows bird who is a thousand times condemned to hell? Surely you can't mean to save someone who has already become

a devil? There is no hope whatsoever of his amendment and he will never do any good unless he is dead. Unless he is destroyed this man will continue to destroy others, for the lives of many have been in danger because of his wicked life.' The holy father replied, 'I know, my dear Count, that this is a very evil robber who has fully deserved the most severe torments. Do not think that in doing this I am wanting to let a sinner go unpunished. I prefer to take him away from the executioners and give him a death which he deserves more because it lasts longer. You have ordered that he shall suffer for a short time by a death which ends quickly: I will make him suffer agony daily and endure the longest possible death. You have caught a thief and you only put him on the gibbet for a day or two: I will nail him to the cross for many years, hanging alive under the yoke of punishment.' When that most Christian prince heard this, he was silent and did not dare to contradict the holy father. So that most loving father took off his cloak and put it on his captive and cut his hair into a tonsure, and so he joined him to the flock of the Lord, making a sheep out of a wolf, a convert out of a criminal. The robber came with Bernard to Clairvaux where he undertook obedience to death. Unless I am mistaken, he lived more than thirty years in the Order. He was called Constantius and I have seen and known him.

(Herbert, 11, 15, col. 1324-1325)

NOTES

1. David Knowles, *Christian Monasticism*, New York 1969, ch. 5, p. 77.

2. Boswell's *Life of Johnson*, ed. G.B. Hill, Oxford 1934, vol. 11, p. 166.

3. Eadmer, *Vita Anselmi*, ed. R.W. Southern, Oxford Medieval Texts (reprinted 1972).

4. P. Brown, *Augustine of Hippo: a Biography*, Faber and Faber, 1967.

5. *S. Bernardi Opera Omnia*, ed. J. Leclercq et al., 9 vols., Rome, 1957; *Vita Prima S. Bernardi*, ed. J.P. Migne, *Patrologia Latinae Cursus Completus CLXXXV*, Paris, 1833.

6. On the influence of the desert tradition on the early Cistercians see Etienne Gilson, *The Mystical Theology of St. Bernard*, London, 1940, pp. 17-19.

7. Translations of the *Apophthegmata* in English may be found in *The Sayings of the Desert Fathers*, tr. Benedicta Ward, Mowbrays, 1975. Other translations are listed in the bibliography given there.

8. B. Ward, *Sayings of the Desert Fathers*, Mowbrays, 1975, p. 2.

9. Op. cit., p. 117.

10. *Vita Prima S. Bernardi, P.L.* CLXXXV, col. 283.

11. Herbertus, *De Miraculis, P.L.* CLXXXV, cols. 1274-1384.

12. Conradus, *Exordium Magnum Cisterciense*, ed. B. Greisser, Rome, 1961.

13. *Vita Prima S. Bernardi, P.L.* CLXXXV, col. 356.

NOTES ON CONTRIBUTORS

JEAN LECLERCQ OSB is a monk of Clervaux in Luxembourg. He has been pre-eminent among historians of medieval monasticism for many years and is known throughout the world through his books, articles and lectures. He has recently completed the definitive edition of the works of St Bernard of Clairvaux.

ANDREW LOUTH is Chaplain of Worcester College and lecturer in patristic theology in the University of Oxford.

MARTIN SMITH SSJE is a member of the Society of St John the Evangelist. He is a graduate of Worcester College, and is at present preparing a doctoral thesis on modern trinitarian theology.

ROWAN WILLIAMS holds a doctorate from Oxford University for his thesis on the theology of Vladimir Lossky. He has written several articles and recently published a translation of P. Pascal's *Religion of the Russian People*. He is at present a lecturer at the College of the Resurrection, Mirfield.

BRIAN GOLDING is a graduate of Wadham College, Oxford and is completing a doctoral thesis on the Gilbertines. He is at present a junior research fellow at the University of Exeter.

SISTER ISABEL MARY, SISTER EDMÉE and SISTER BENEDICTA WARD SLG are members of the Community of the Sisters of the Love of God. Benedicta Ward has published several articles on medieval and monastic themes and three volumes of translations of medieval and patristic texts (*The Prayers and Meditations of St Anselm, The Sayings of the Desert Fathers,* and *The Wisdom of the Desert Fathers*).

FAIRACRES PUBLICATIONS

SELECT LIST

FULL LIST OF PUBLICATIONS OBTAINABLE ON REQUEST

NO.		PRICE
12	LEARNING TO PRAY Mother Mary Clare SLG	.15
16	THE VICTORY OF THE CROSS Dumitru Staniloae	.15
21	THE THEOLOGY OF THE RELIGIOUS LIFE: An Anglican Approach A. M. Allchin	.10
24	SILENCE AND PRAYER Mother Mary Clare SLG	.15
26	THE MESSAGE OF SAINT SERAPHIM Irina Gorainov	.15
28	JULIAN OF NORWICH A. M. Allchin and SLG	.35
29	PENTECOST IN THE CHURCH A. M. Allchin	.10
30	ANSELM OF CANTERBURY: A Monastic Scholar, Sister Benedicta SLG	.15
31	PRAYER: ENCOUNTERING THE DEPTHS Mother Mary Clare SLG	.15
40	ST THÉRÈSE OF LISIEUX: Her Relevance for Today Sister Eileen Mary SLG	.15
43	THE POWER OF THE NAME (the Jesus Prayer in Orthodox Spirituality) Kallistos Ware	.25
44	WHOLENESS AND TRANSFIGURATION Illustrated in the Lives of St Francis of Assisi and St Seraphim of Sarov, A. M. Allchin	.15
46	PRAYER AND CONTEMPLATION Robert Llewelyn	.50
48	THE WISDOM OF THE DESERT FATHERS (*The Apophthegmata Patrum*, Anonymous Series), translated by Sister Benedicta SLG	.90
50	THE LETTERS OF ST ANTHONY THE GREAT, translated by Derwas J. Chitty	.50
55	THEOLOGY AND SPIRITUALITY Andrew Louth	.35
57	THE BEAUTY OF HOLINESS: An Introduction to Six Seventeenth-Century Anglican Writers, R. W. Southern and others.	.60

PUBLICATIONS BY GILBERT SHAW

A PILGRIM'S BOOK OF PRAYERS	£1.20
SITIO (I THIRST) Intercessory Prayers	.90
THE CHRISTIAN SOLITARY	.15

OBTAINABLE FROM (postage extra): SLG PRESS, Convent of the Incarnation, Fairacres, Oxford, OX4 1TB